East End Photos
Through Mayar's Eyes
Photo Album: Voluntary Sector 1992-1993

MAYAR AKASH

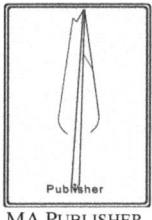

MA PUBLISHER

Copyright © Mayar Akash 2020

Published by MA Publishing (Penzance)
Published October 2020
ISBN-13: 978-1-910499-62-7

All rights reserved. No part of this publication may be reproduced, stored in a retrieval system, or transmitted, in any form or by any means, electronic, mechanical, photocopying, recording, public performances or otherwise, without prior written permission of the copyright holder, except for brief quotations embodied in critical articles or reviews.

Cover designed by Mayar Akash
Typeset in Times New Roman
All photos belong to Mayar Akash

 Paper printed on is FSC Certified, lead free, acid free, buffered paper made from wood-based pulp. Our paper meets the ISO 9706 standard for permanent paper. As such, paper will last several hundred years when stored.

Introduction

This photo book featuring the photographs I've taken during my work at the youth project based in Whitechapel, Davenant Centre, the Progressive Youth Organisation (PYO) in 1992; with my compact camera

These photos were taken with 35mm film, so they don't have the date & time imprint in the image data. However, some of the photos have the date & time imprinted in the photographs through the cameras that I used to start off my photography passion.

For many years I didn't know what to do with them but now it seem fit to organise them like an albums and publish them, give access to the world, to see the East End through a Bangladeshi, Sylheti living in Tower Hamlets, with the urban factor; no hold bars assimilation into the Cockney East End, way of life.

The photos are not in any particular order, they are all random, I want to give people a taster of random things that I have encounter in my life journey.

"Date & Time stamped photos, I know where I was, do you know where you were in the world?"

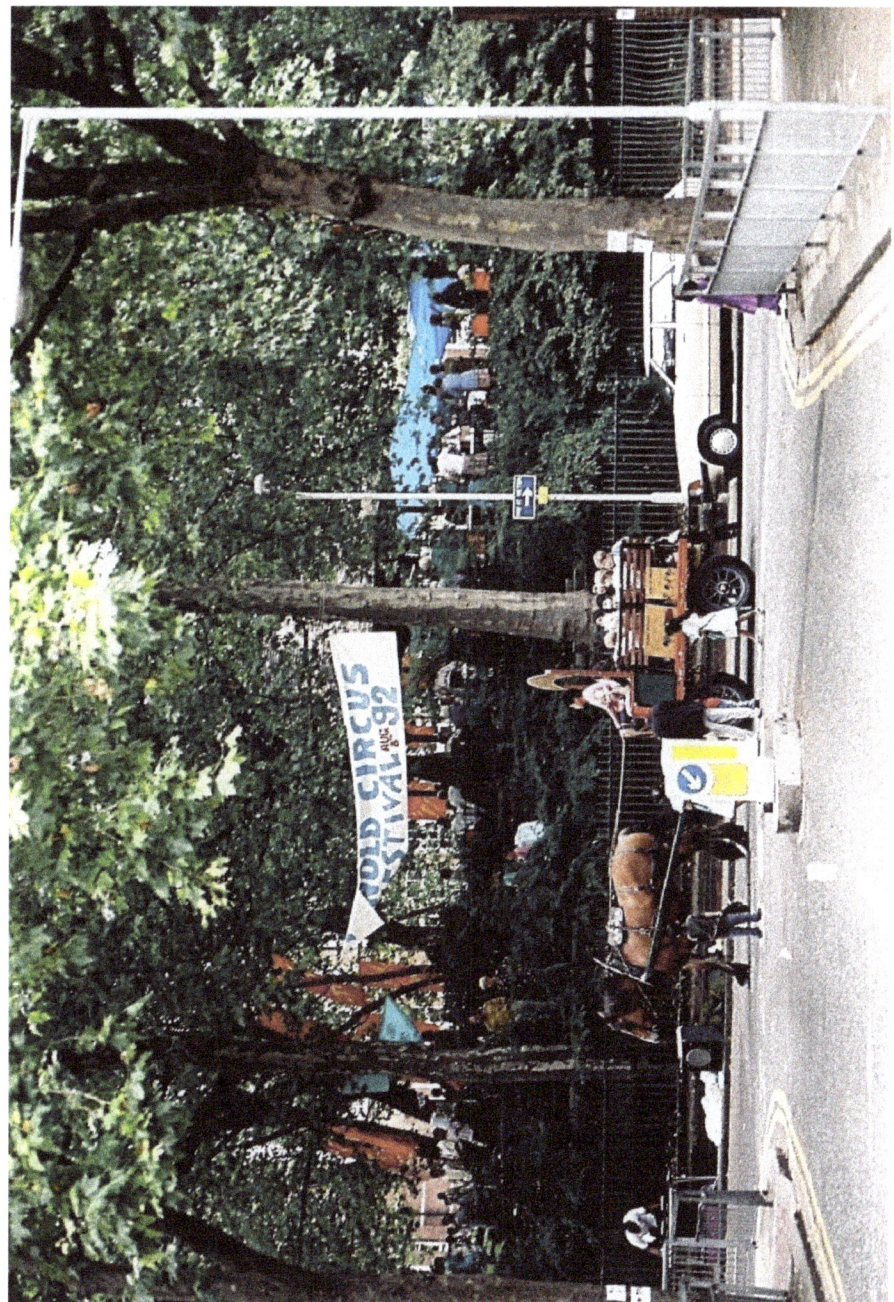

World Circus Festival 8.8.1992, Held on the Bandstand, Arnold Circus, Boundary Estate, E2.

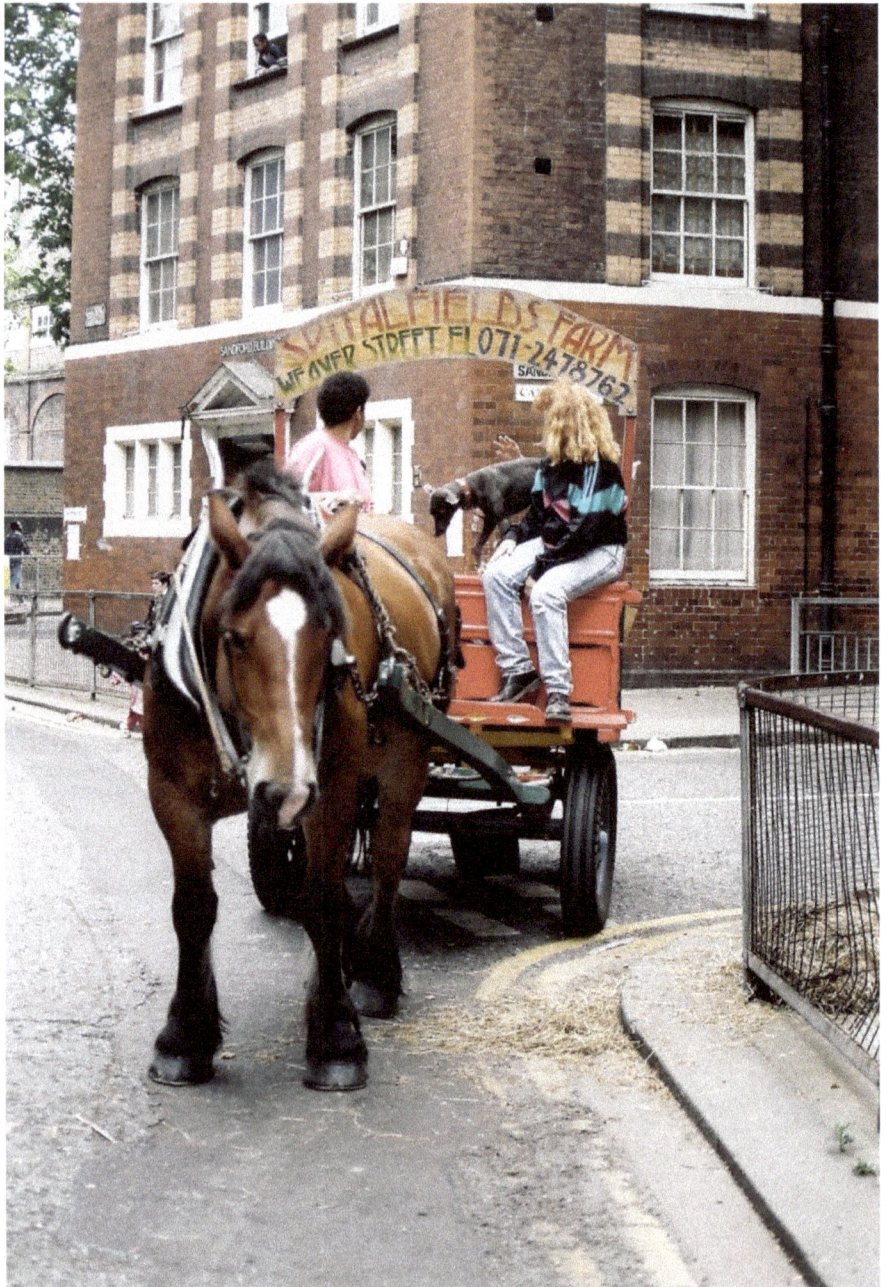

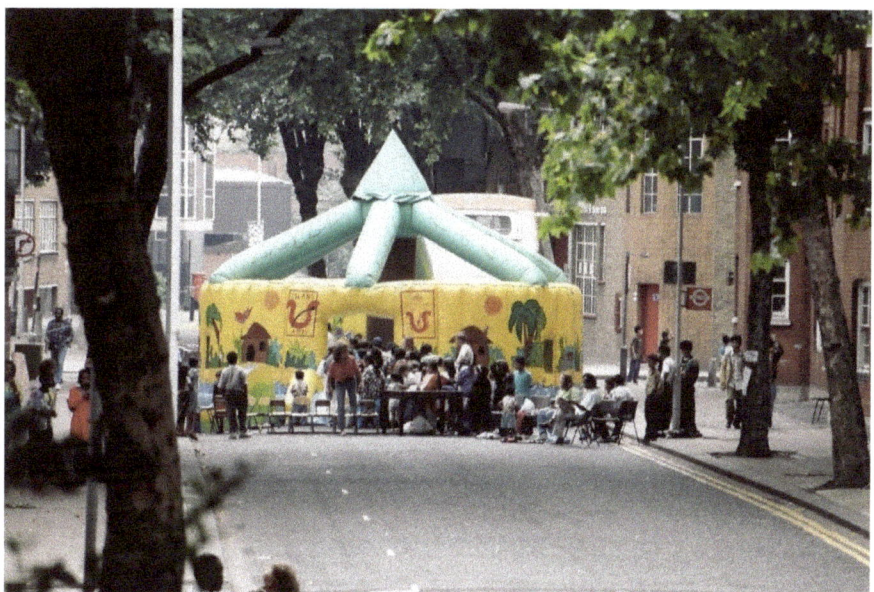

Bouncy Castle and face painting outside St Hilda's East building, on Club Row, with junction of Old Nichol Street.

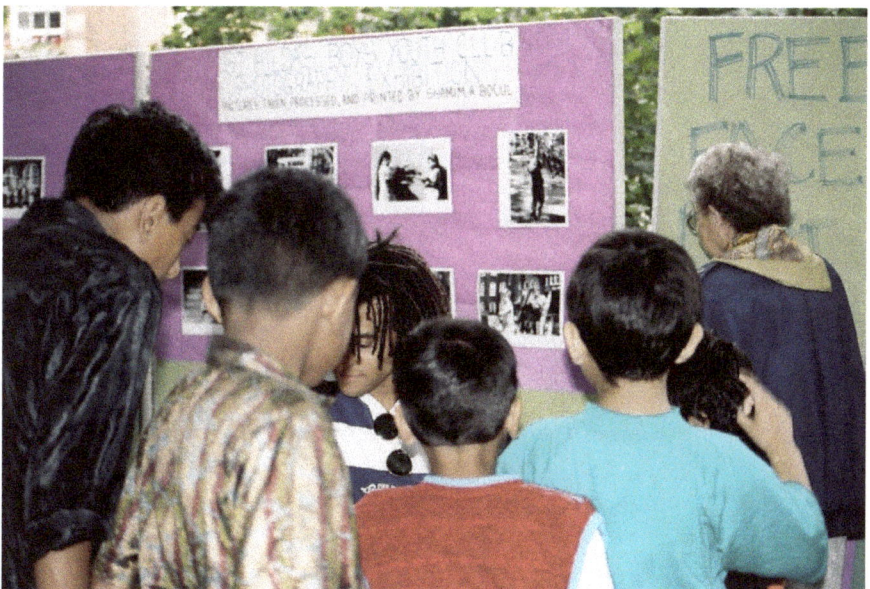

Ray engaging with the local boys, behind Ray in a Photo exhibition, displaying photos by Shamim and Bocul from boundary estate.

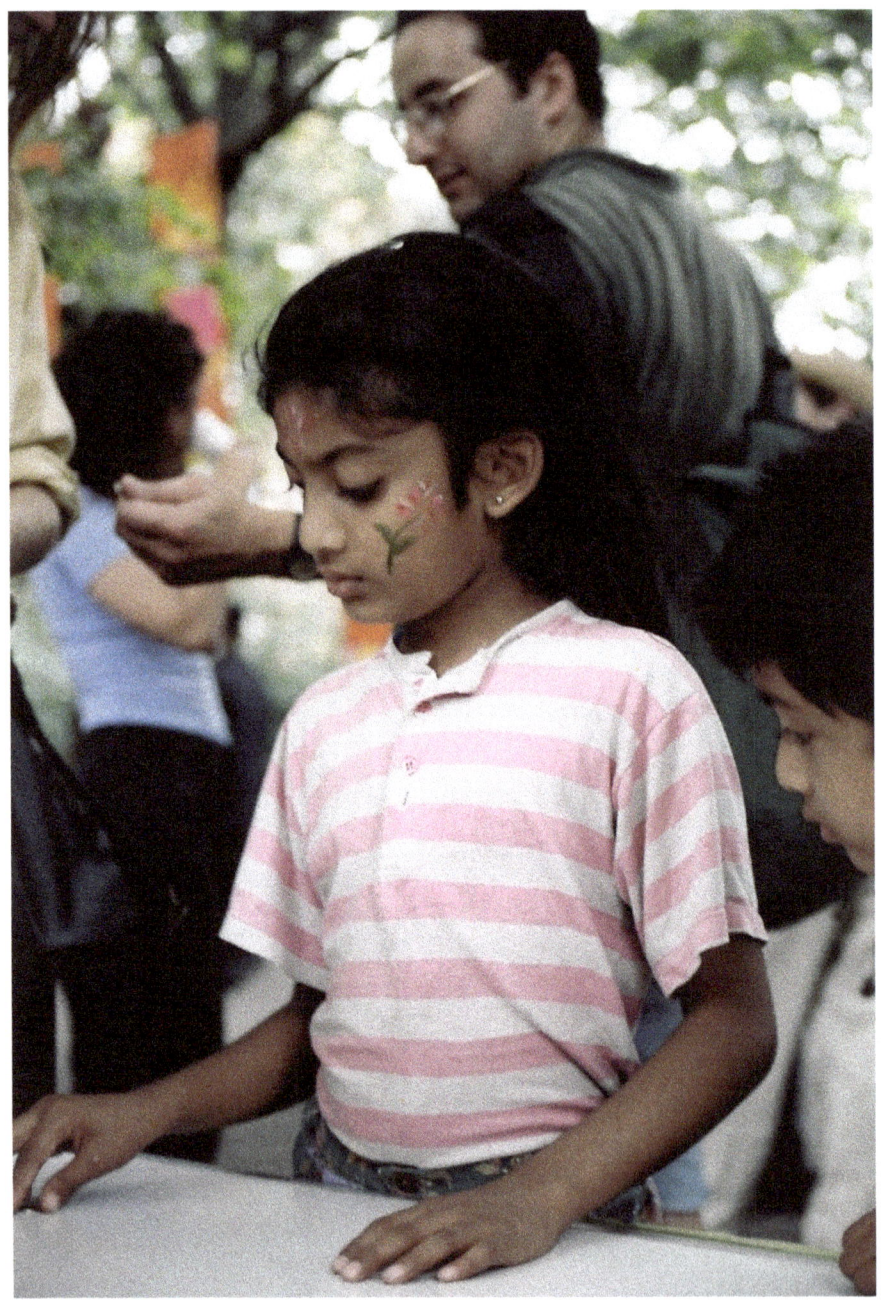

Local girls and boys taking active part in the event

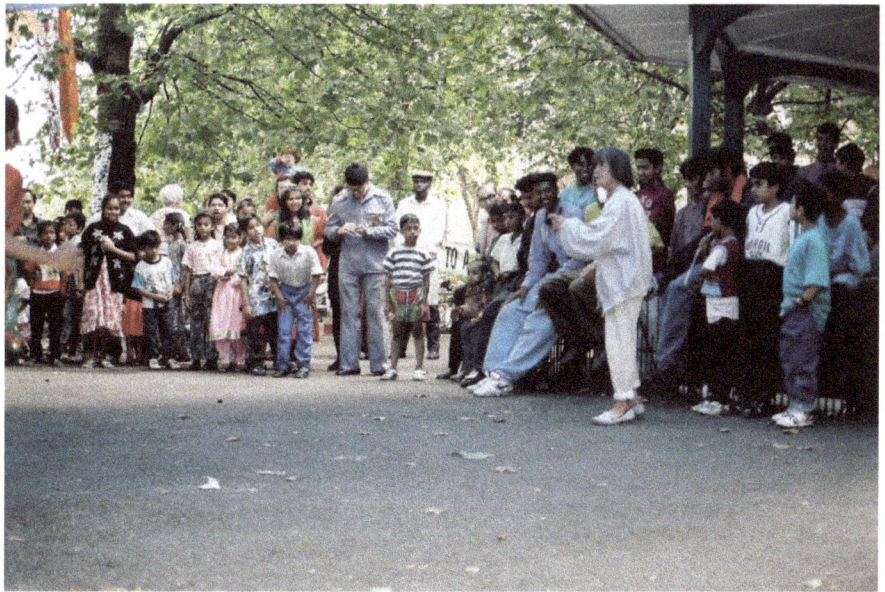

Local residents engaging in the event

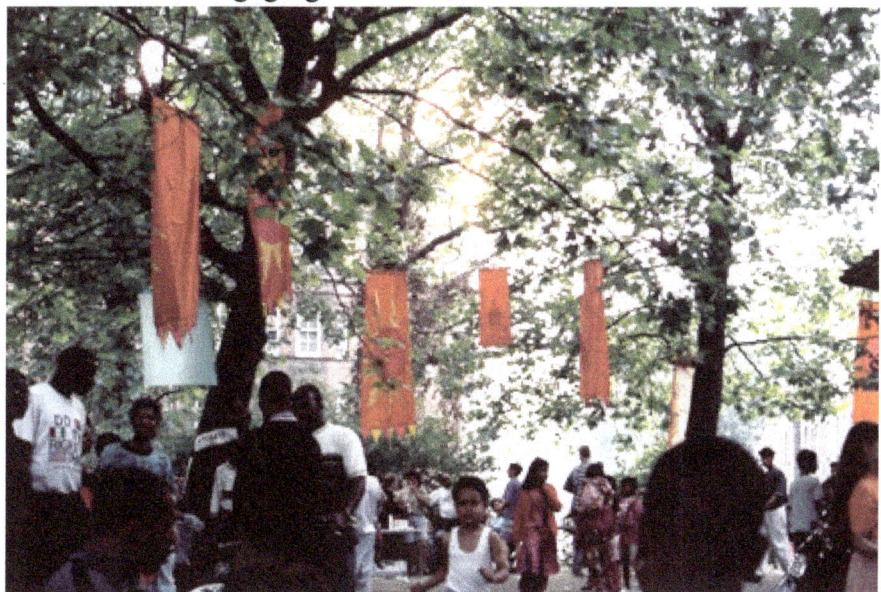

All section of the community have come out to enjoy fun day.

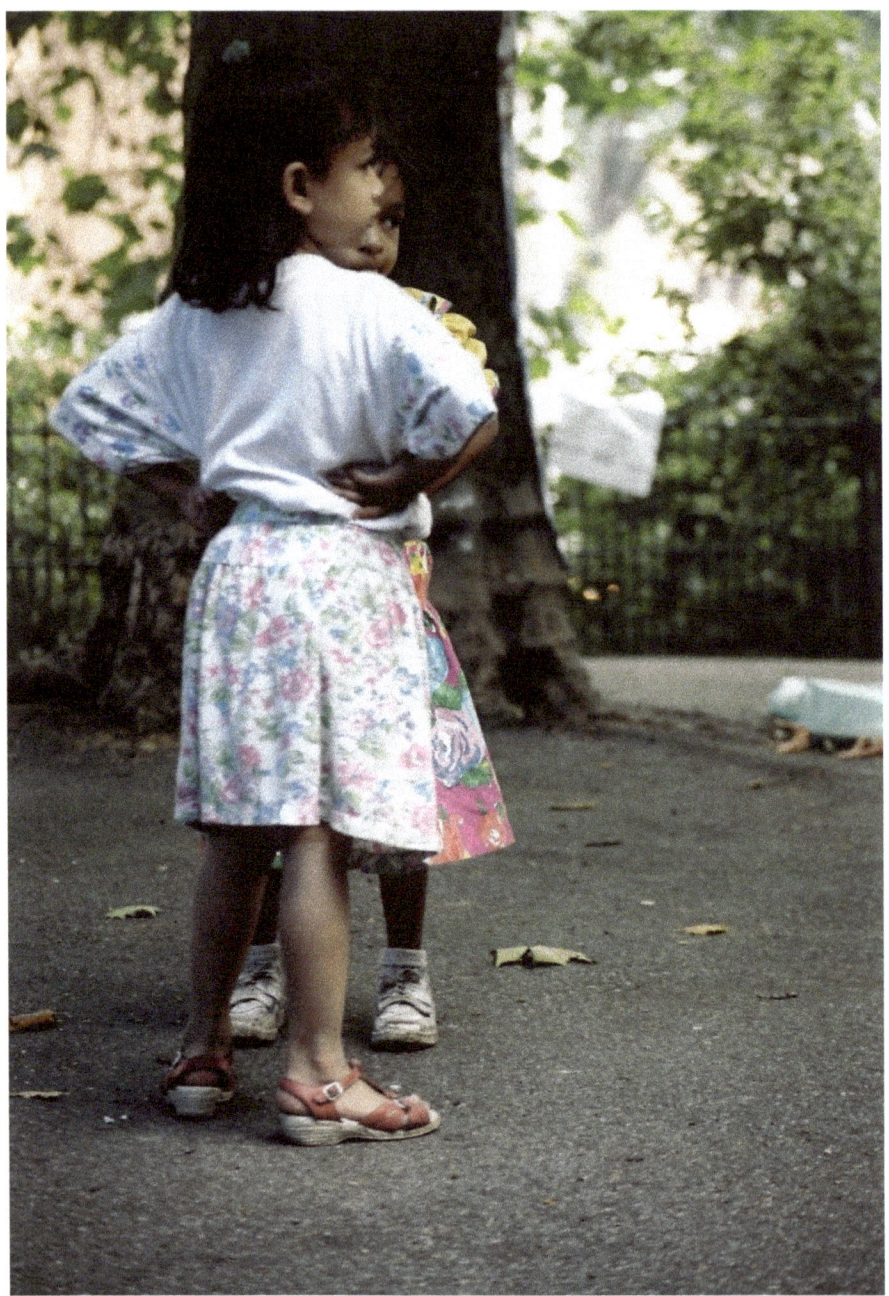

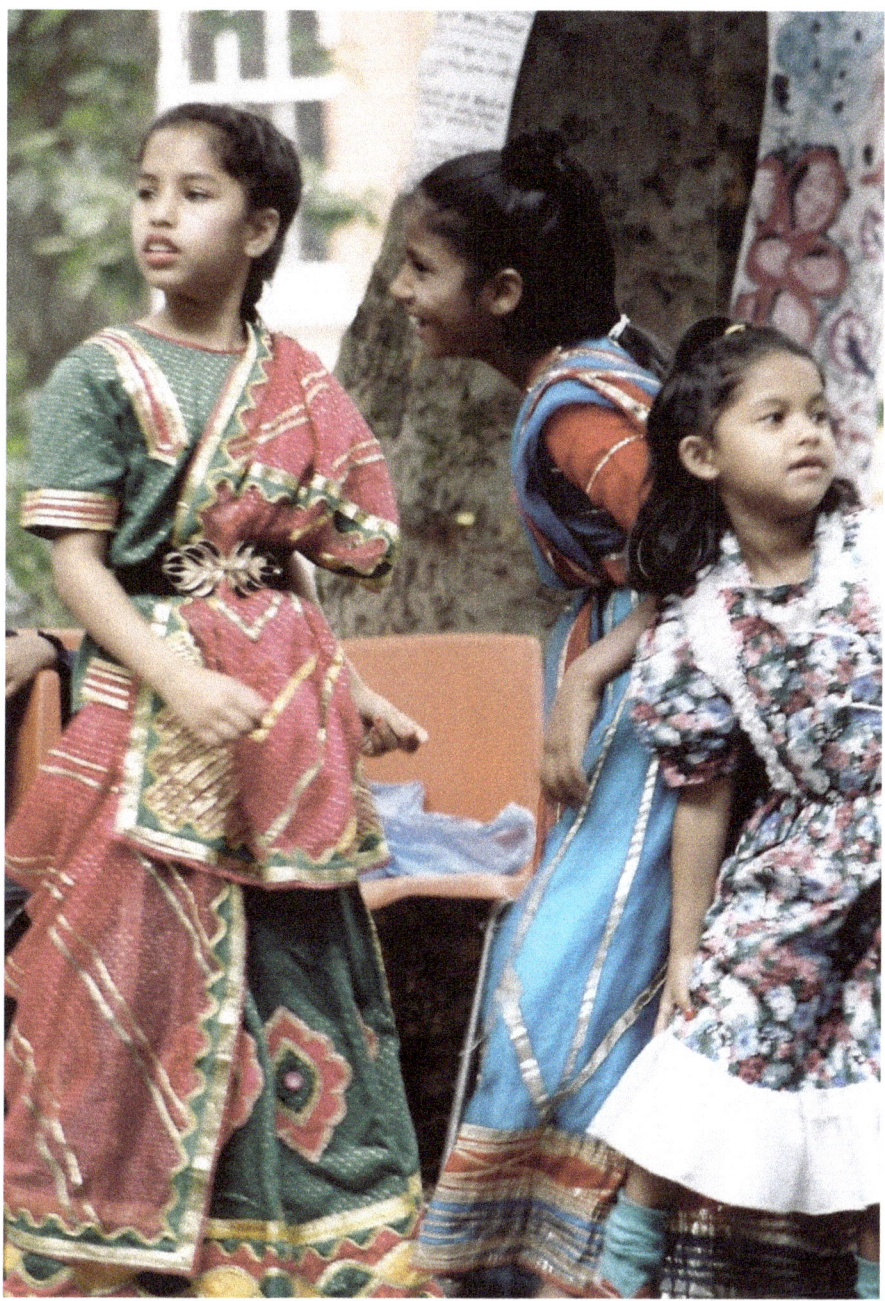

Brave little performers

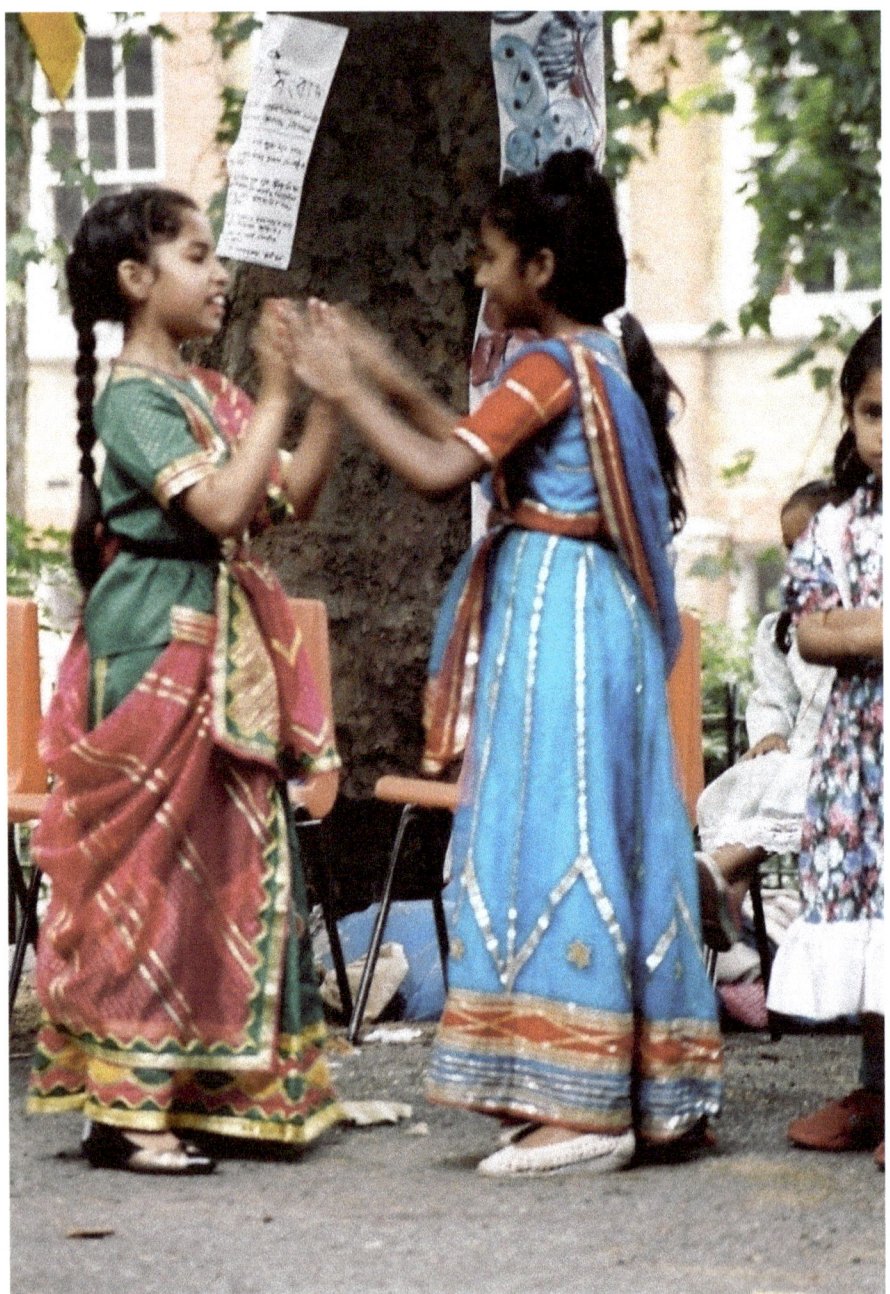

Warming up

East End Photos, Through Mayar's Eyes : Voluntary Sector 1992-1993

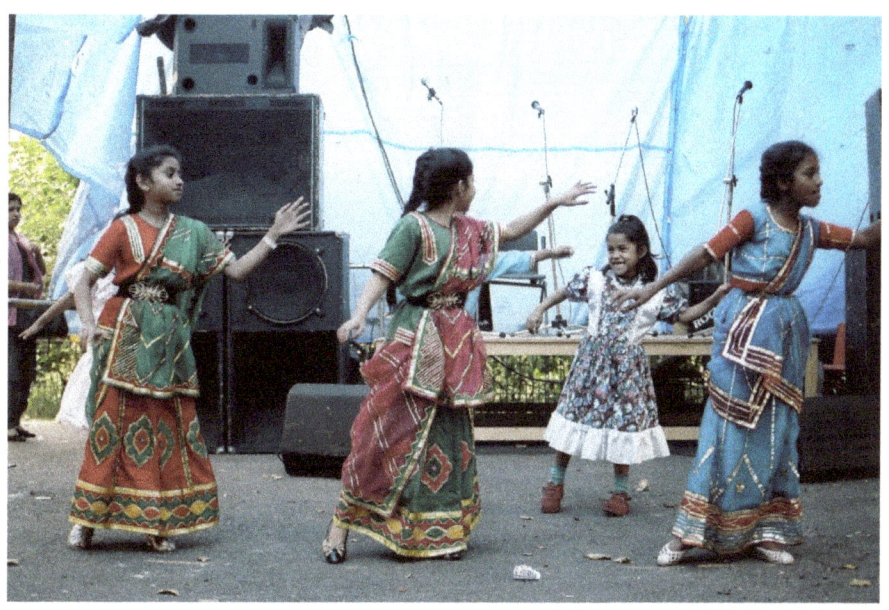

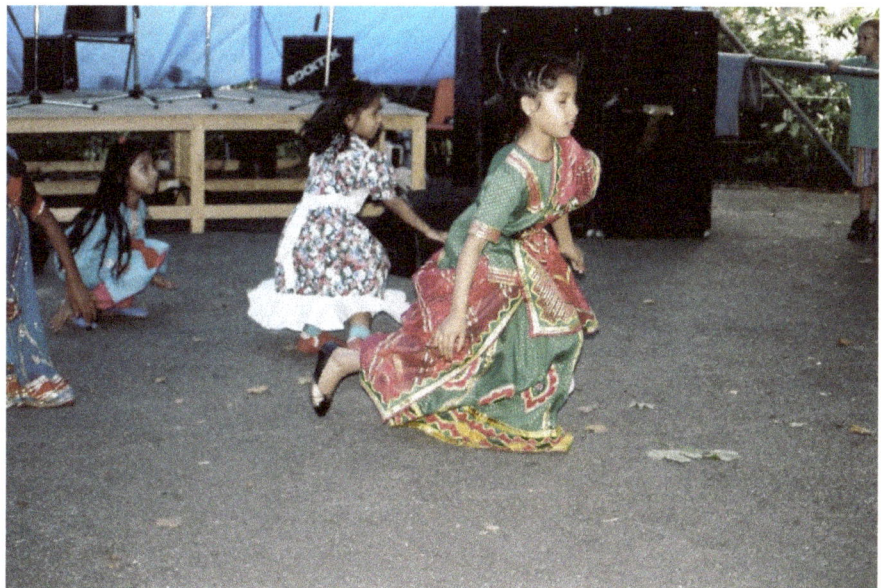

Performing their dance routine

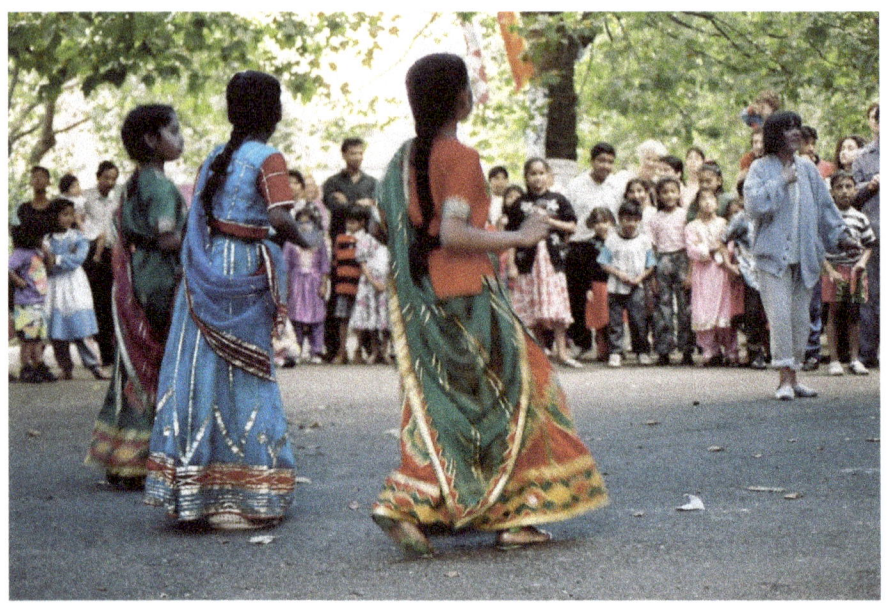
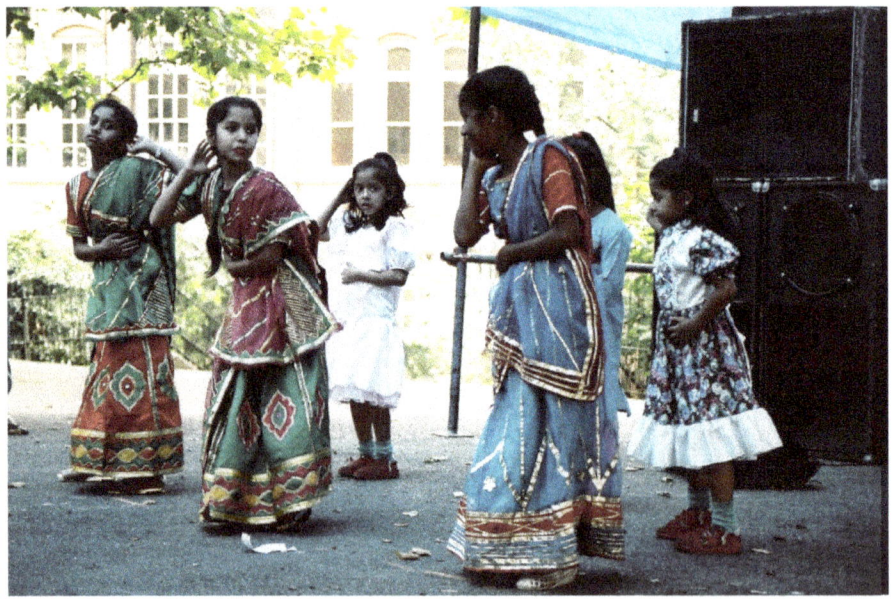

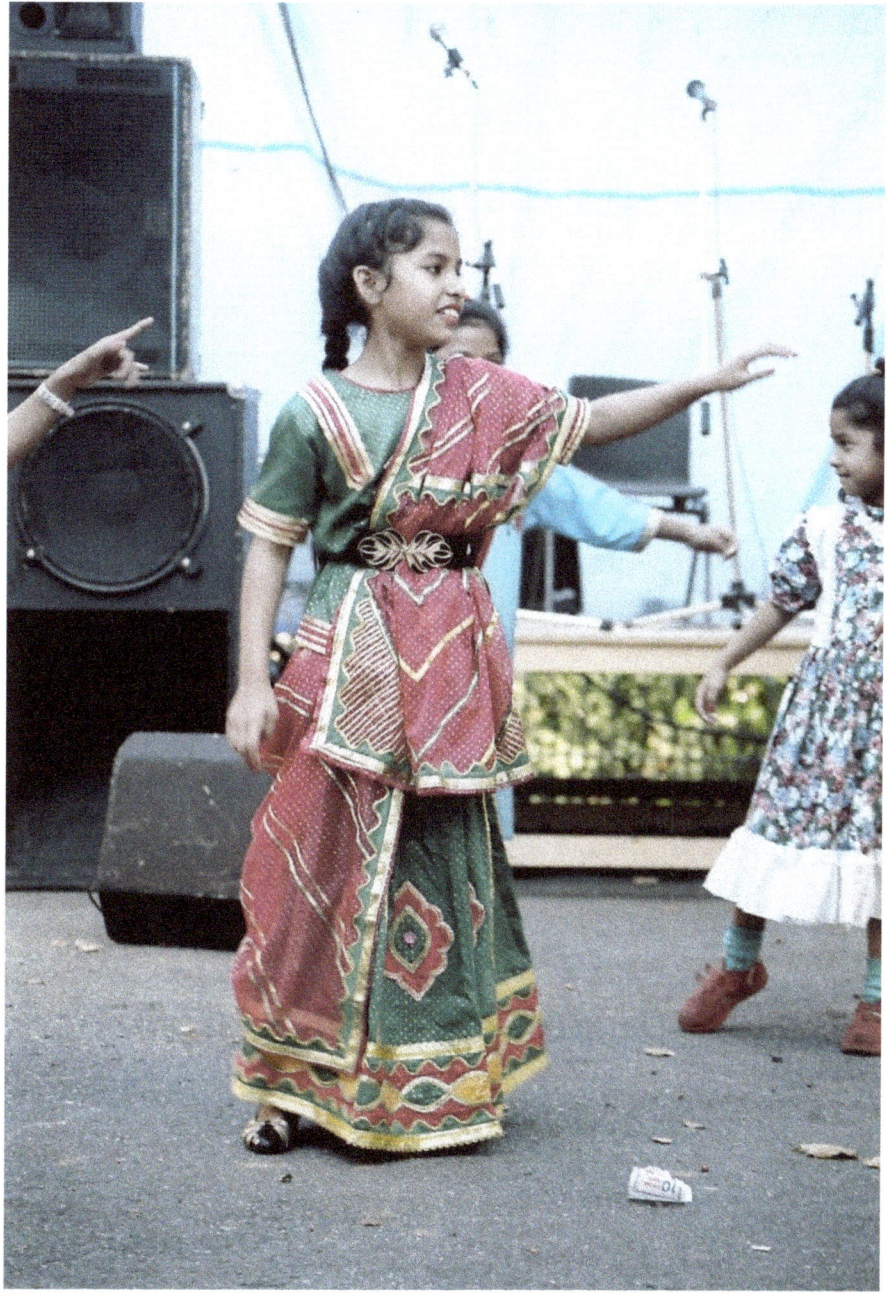

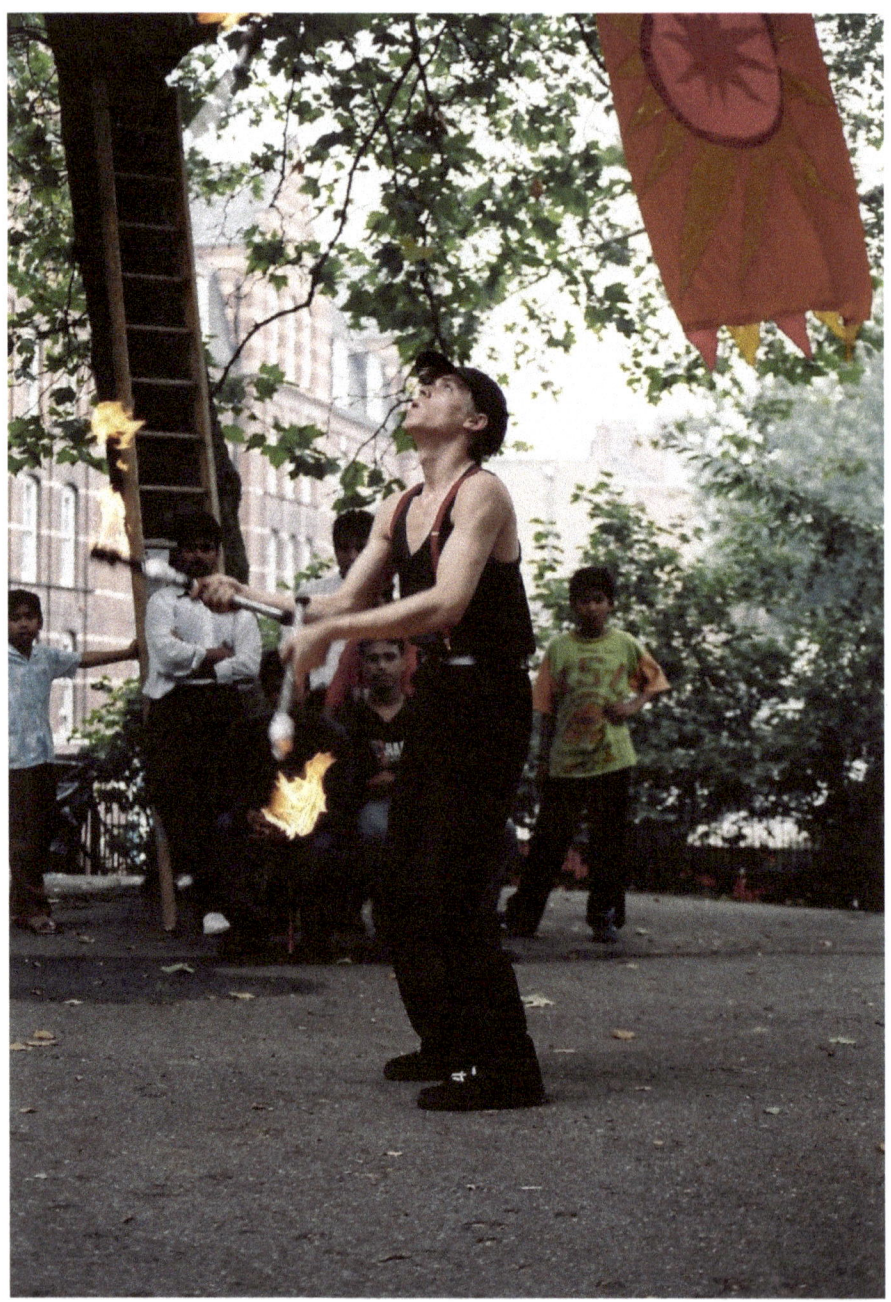

The fire juggler!

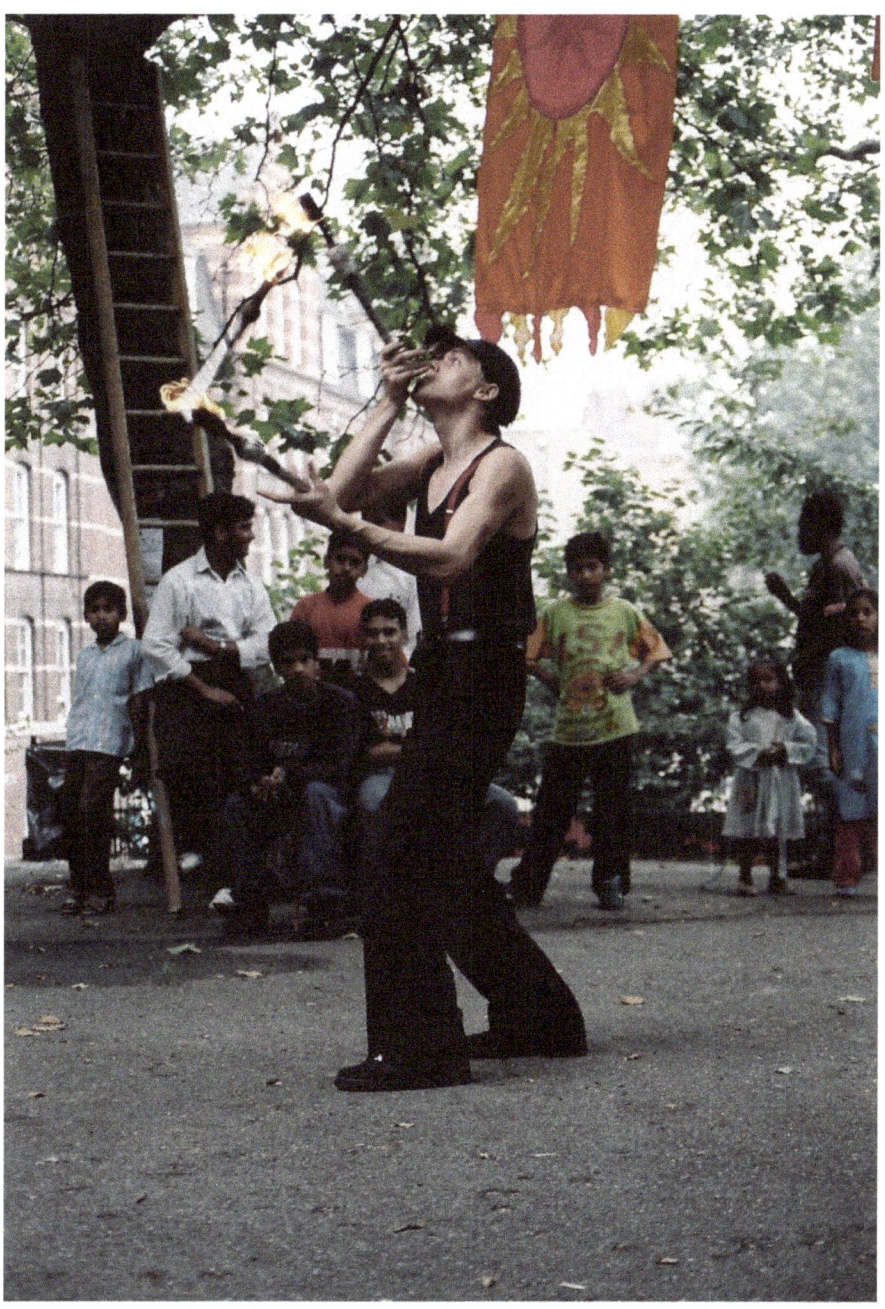

In his mouth

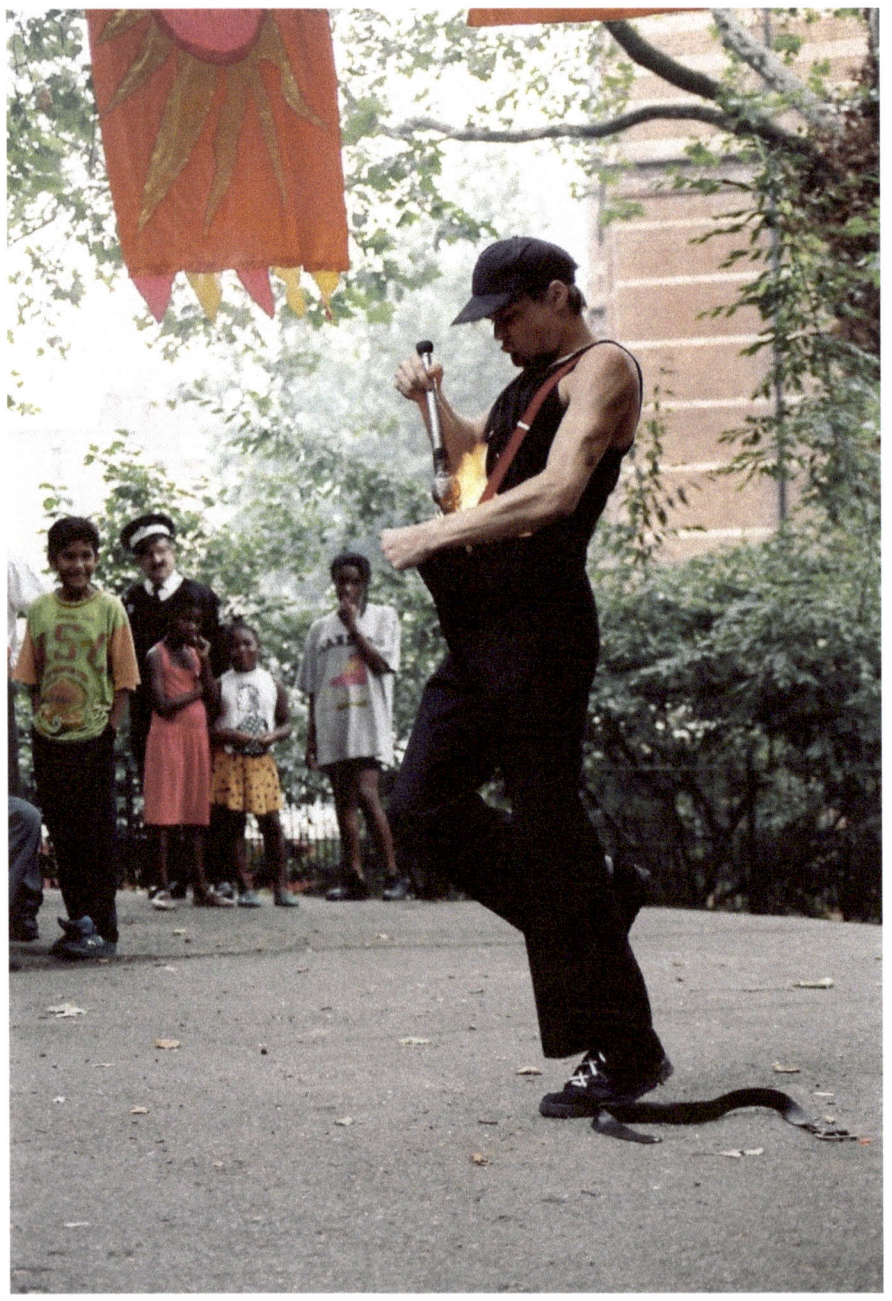

In his pants, St Johns Ambulance man ready in the background.

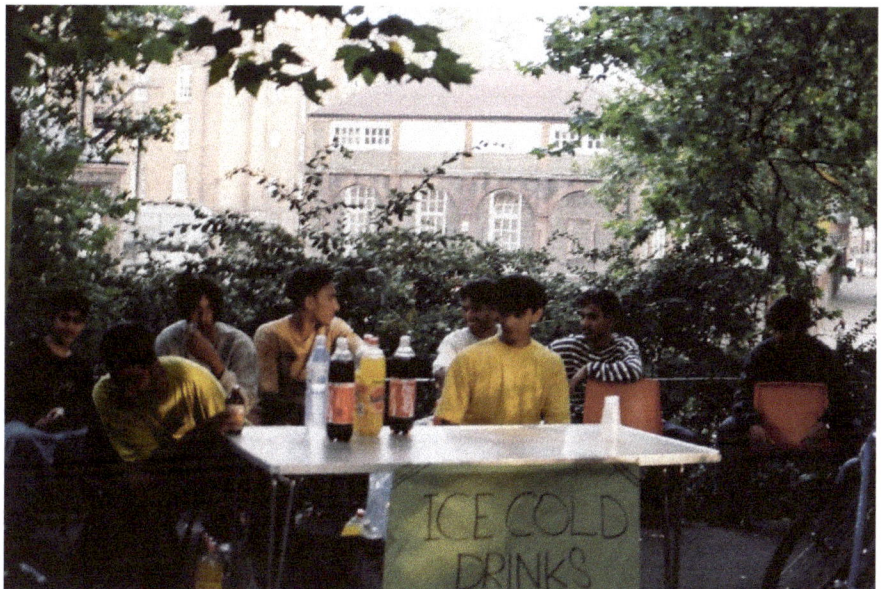
Local youth group (PYO) selling refreshments (me in the yellow).

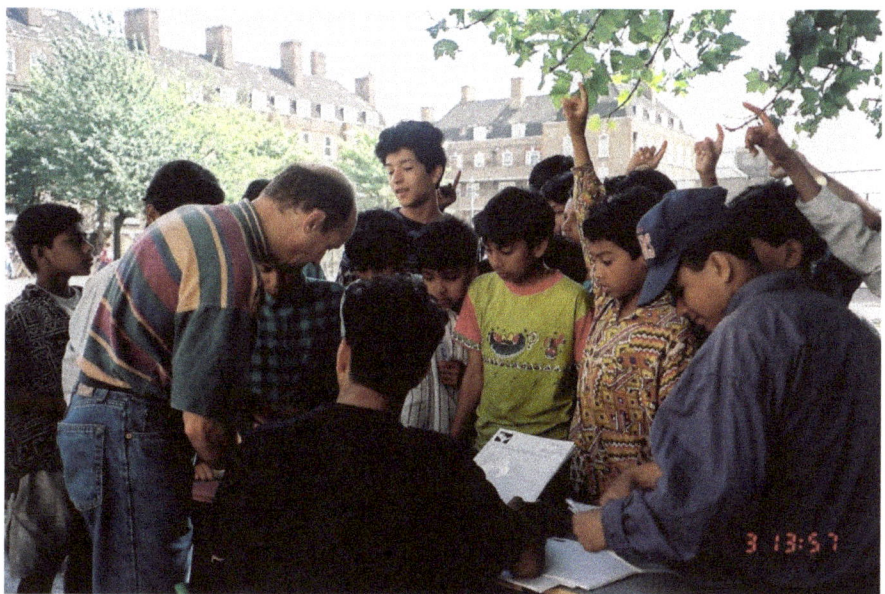
Now we are going around the borough, we now in Collingwood Estate, off Brady Street, PYO's Detached Street Projects' summer holiday fun day. David Holloway and Abjol Miah taking registration.

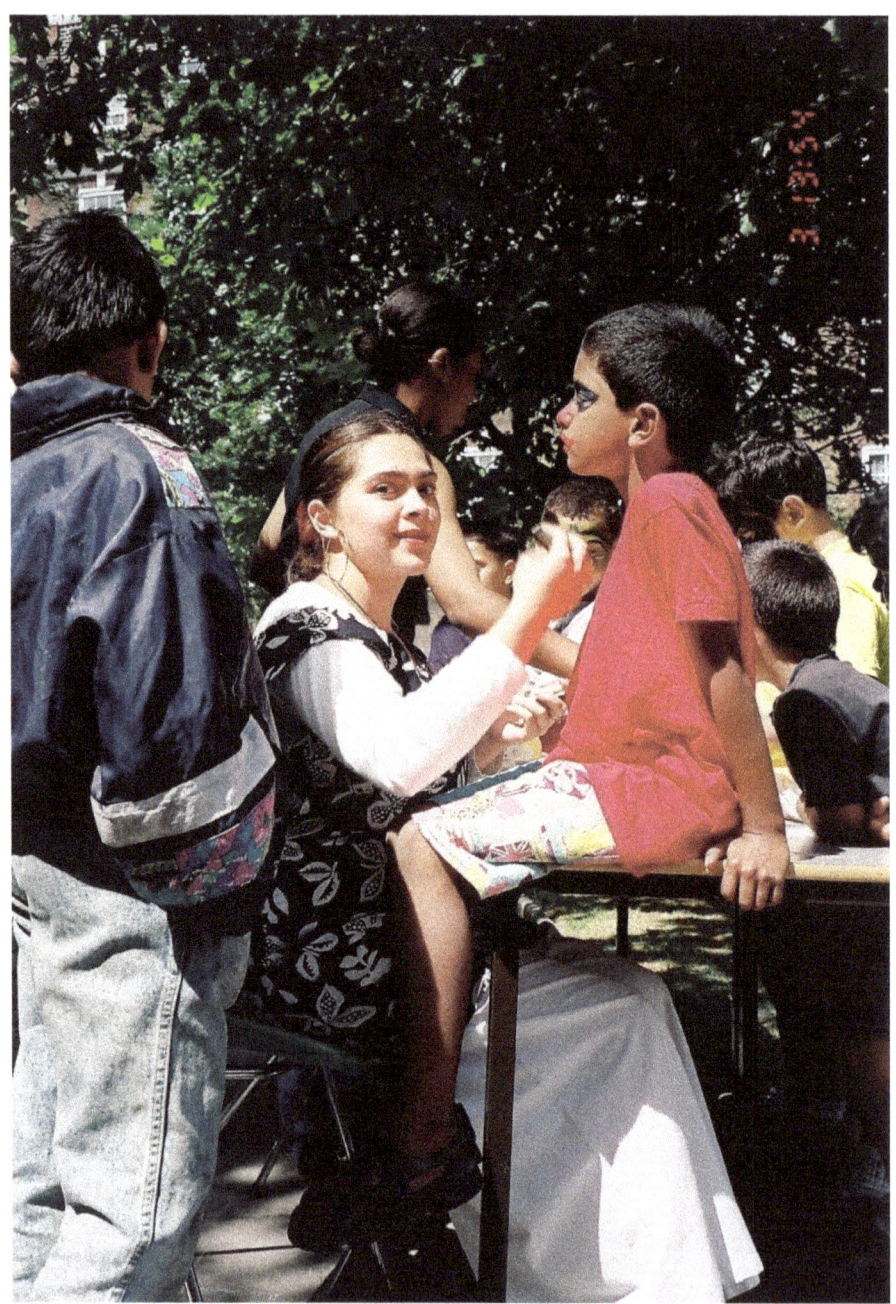

Sophie, PYO Member helping with the face painting 3.8.1992

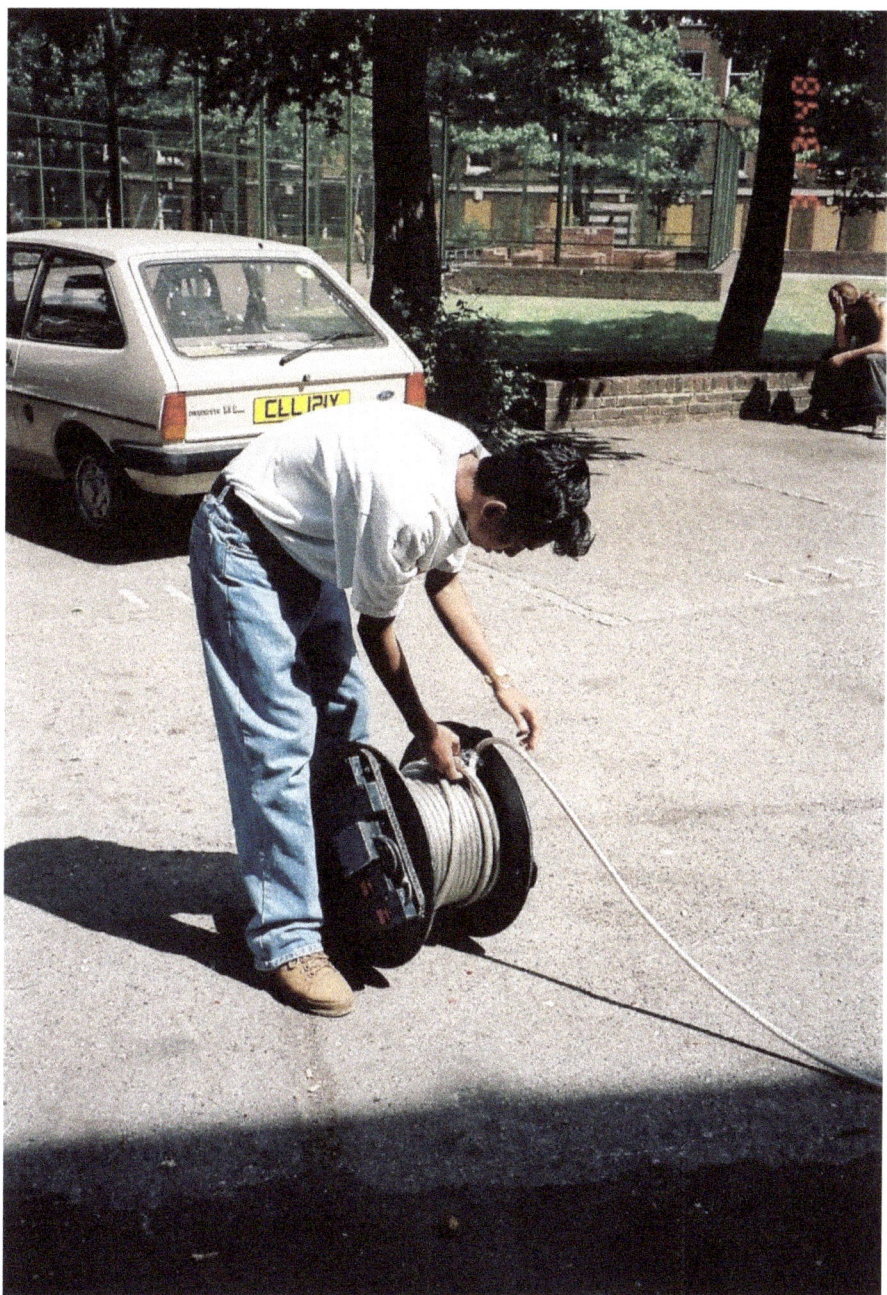

Collingwood Youth Forum and PYO members helping to set up the event.

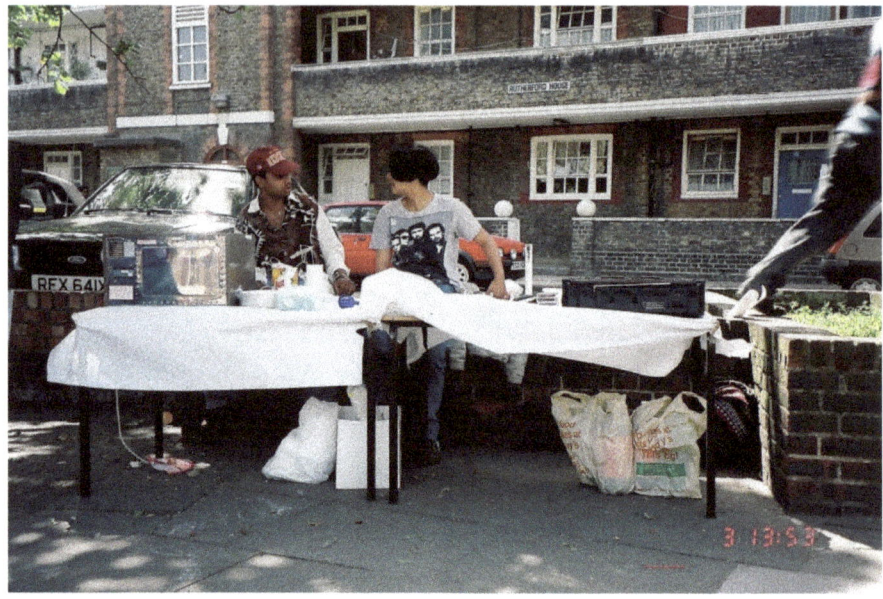

Refreshments sorted.

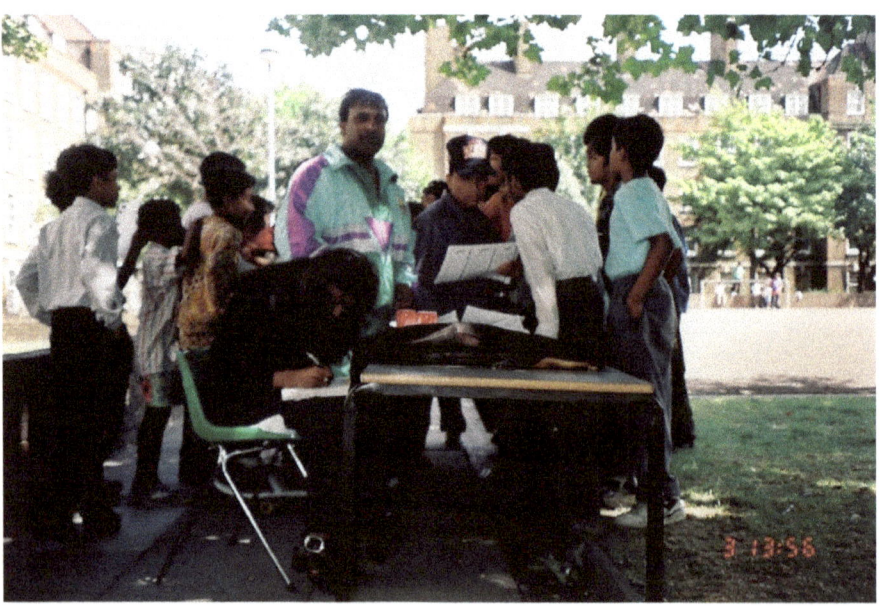

East End Photos, Through Mayar's Eyes : Voluntary Sector 1992-1993

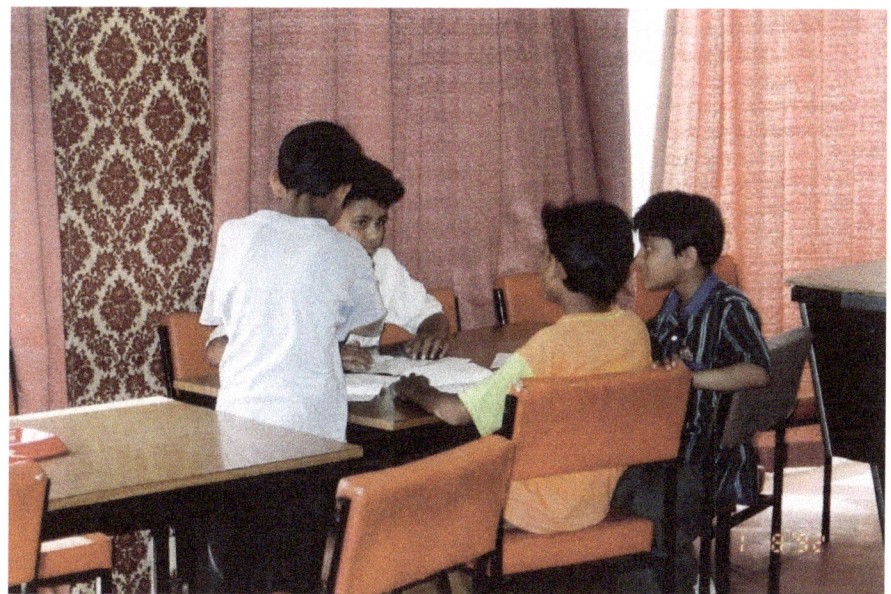

CYF - in the tenants hall room, taking part in activity

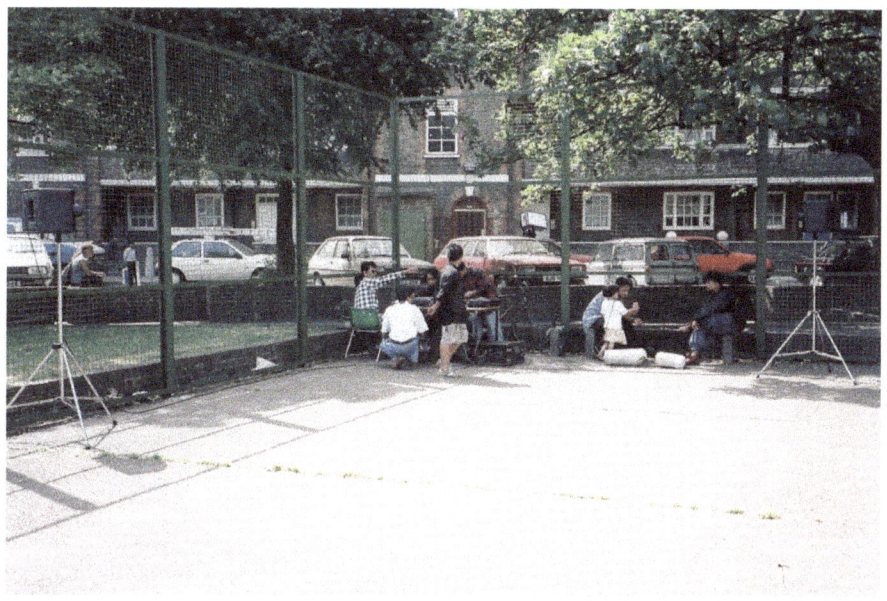

Sound System installed in the pitch for the music.

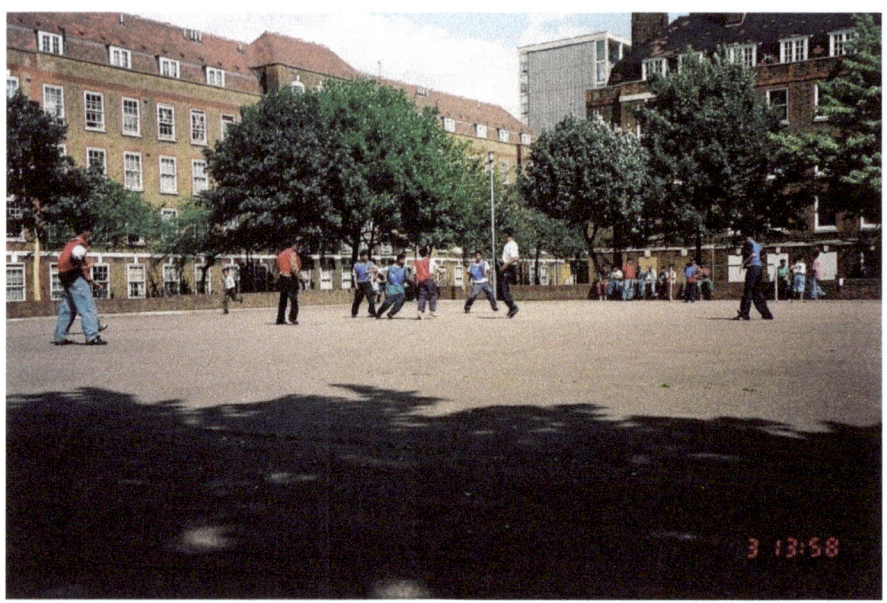

Football tournament taking place

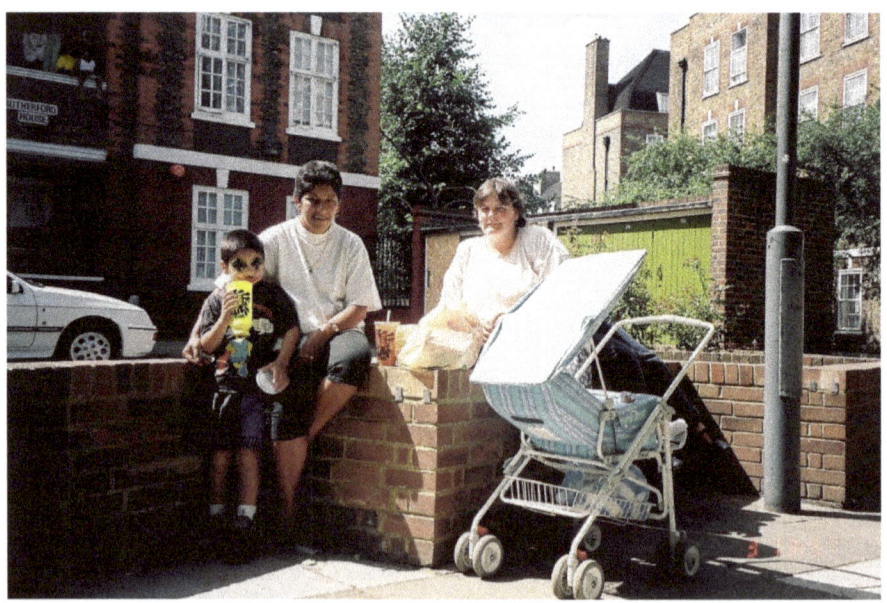

Local parents out enjoying the lovely day with their children.

Davenant centre, Whitechapel Road

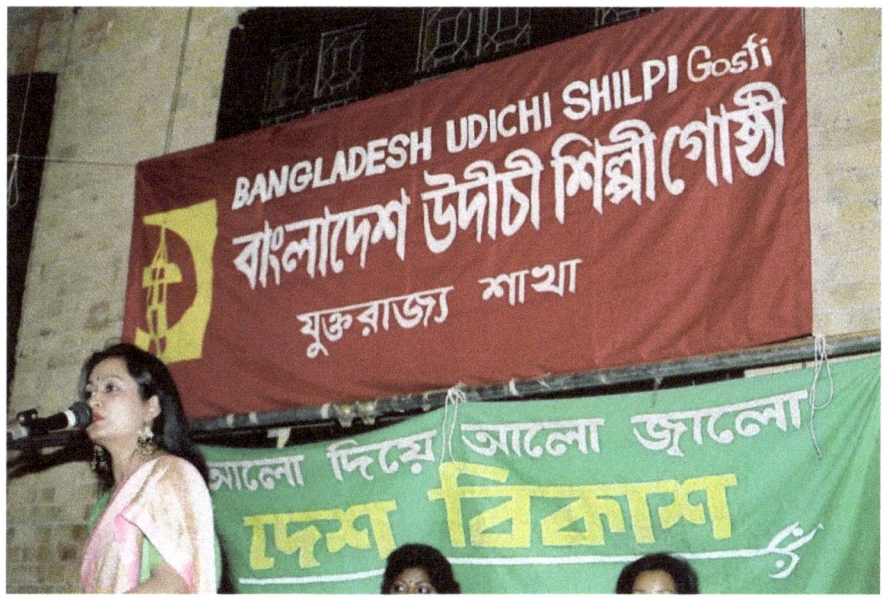

Cultural Event taking place at the Davenant Centre Hall, Whitechapel.

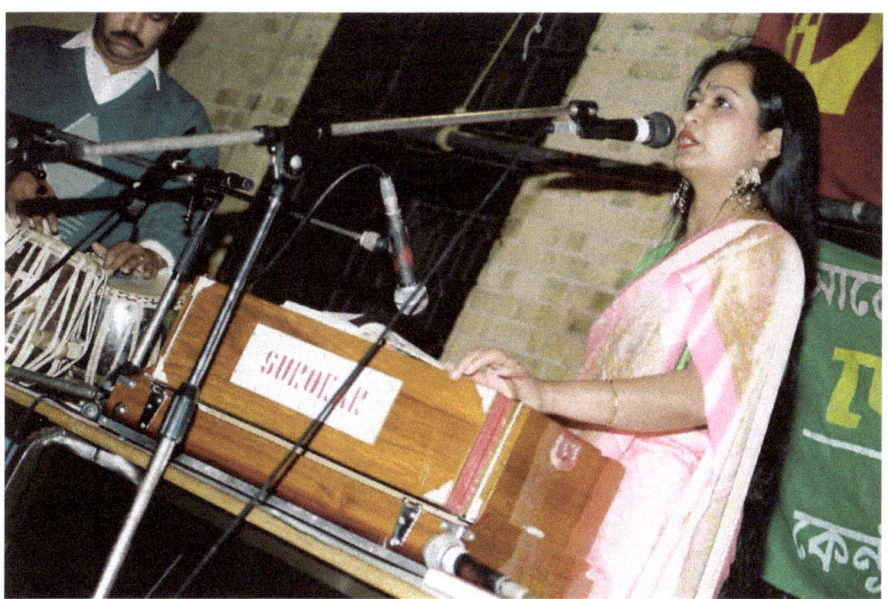

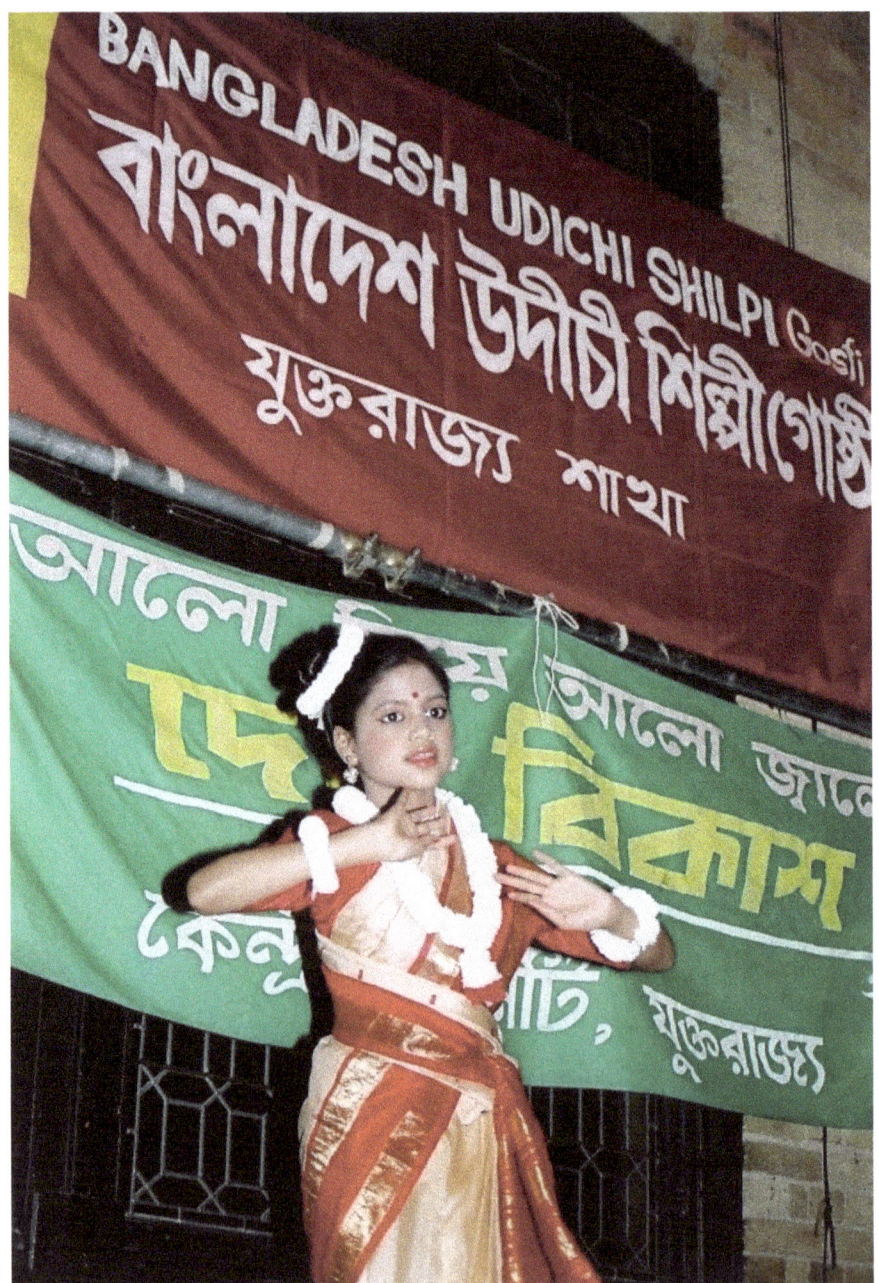

Young dancer displaying her cultural moves, convey the story.

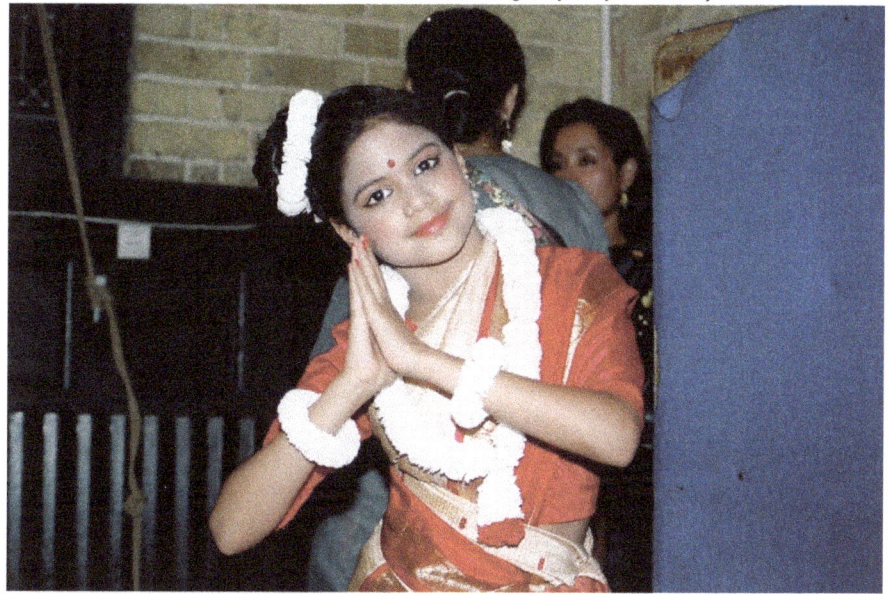

Shamim Azad in the back ground, over-looking the event from the Davenant management Committee.

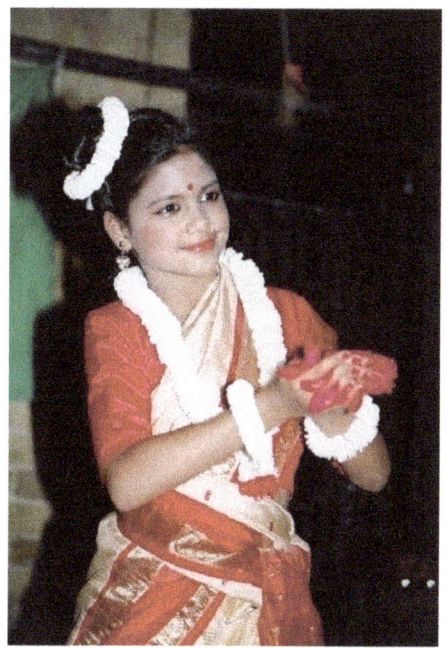 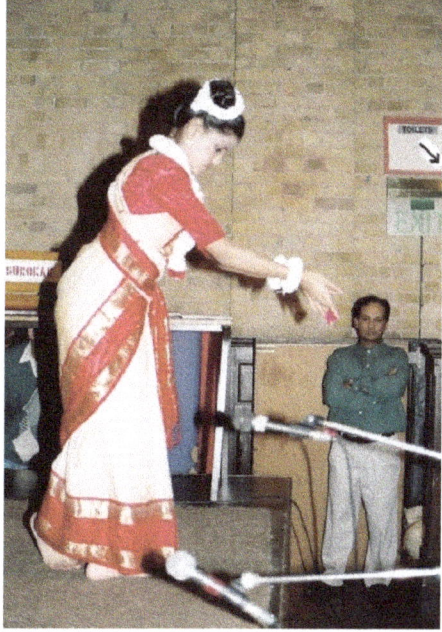

With rose petals in her hands - she drops them as way of welcoming the audience.

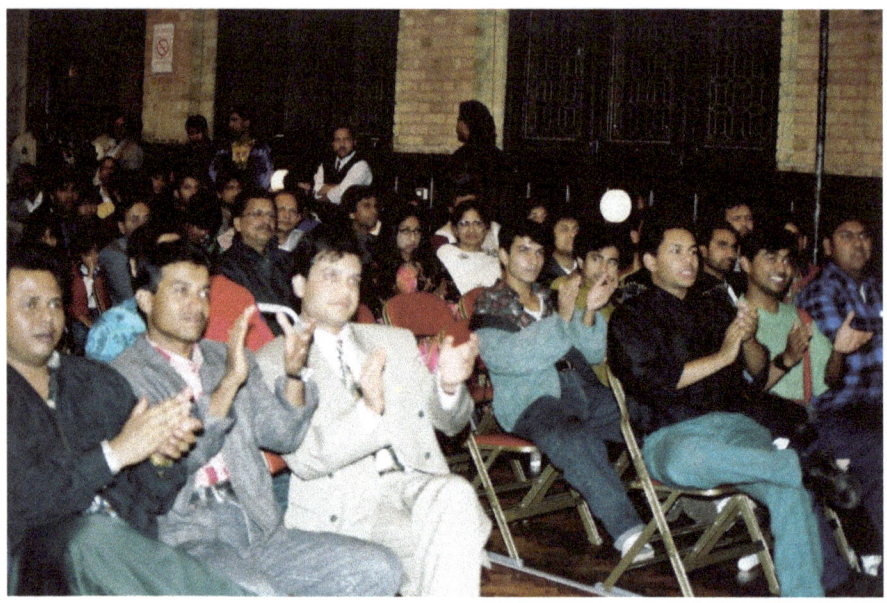

Local community audience, enjoying the event.

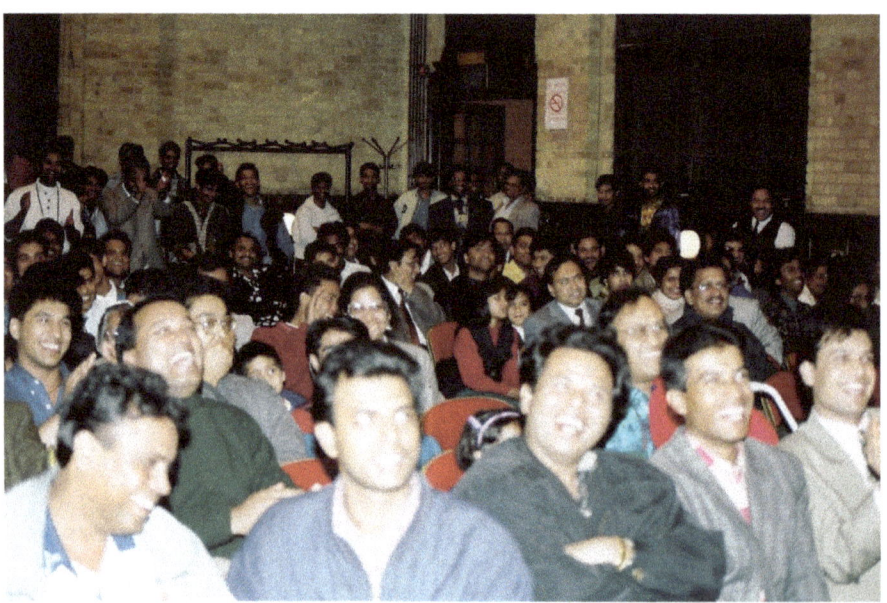

PYO hosting German group in the club upstairs at the Davenant Centre. 7.2.1992

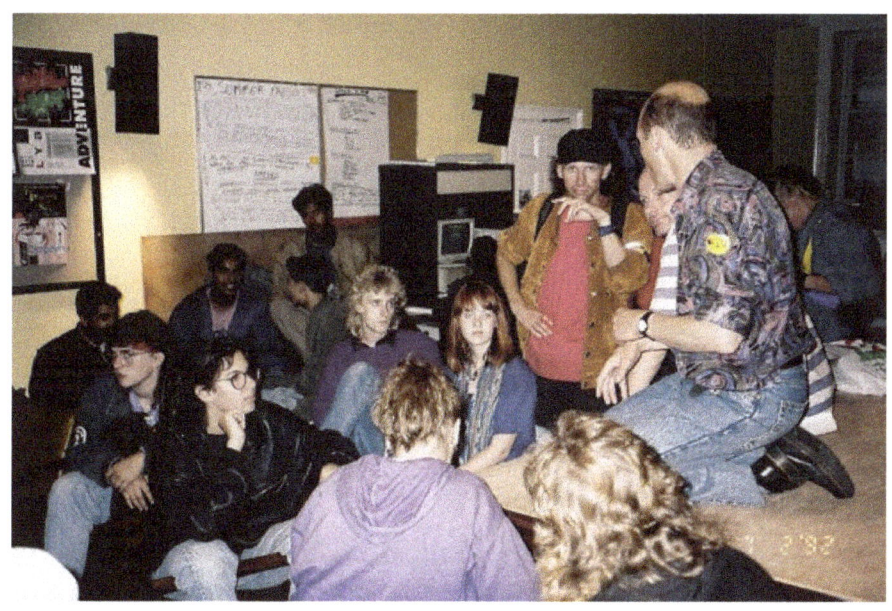

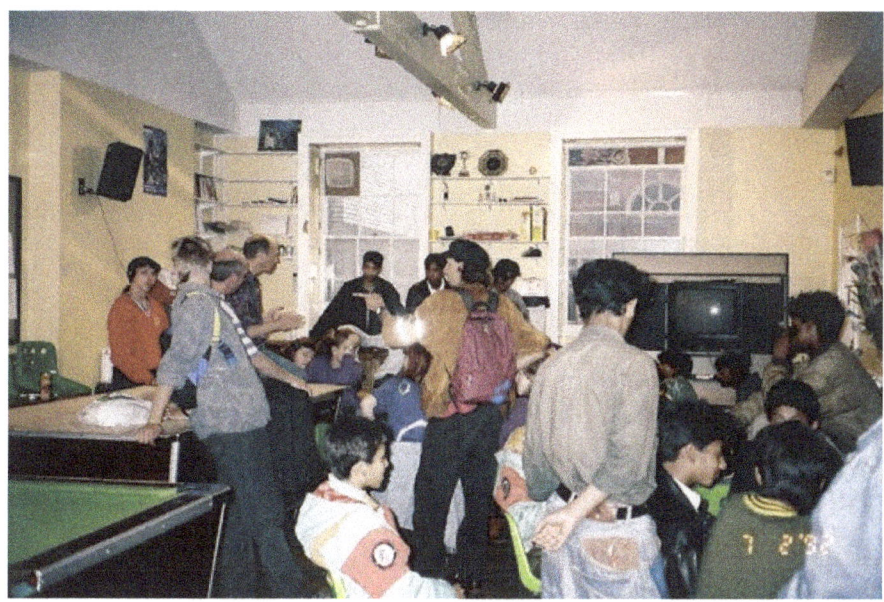

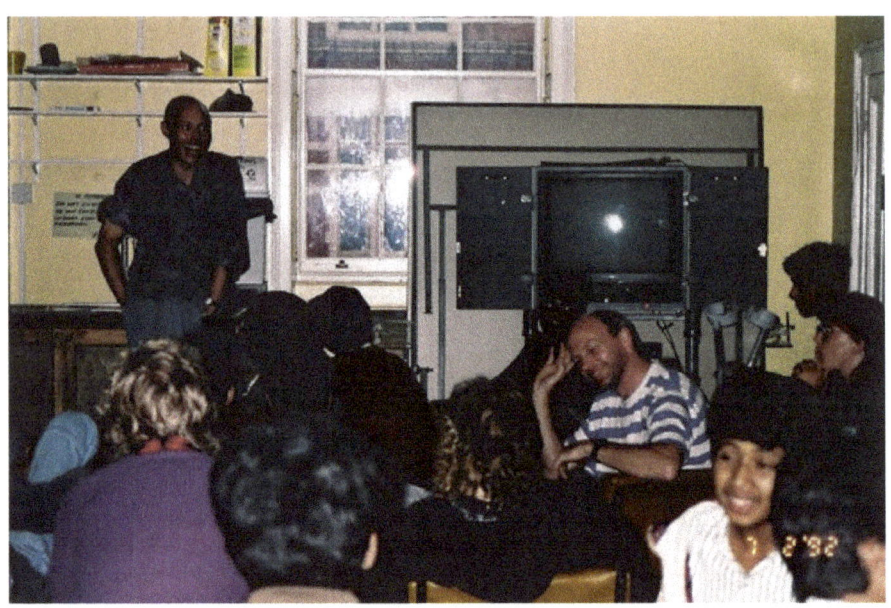

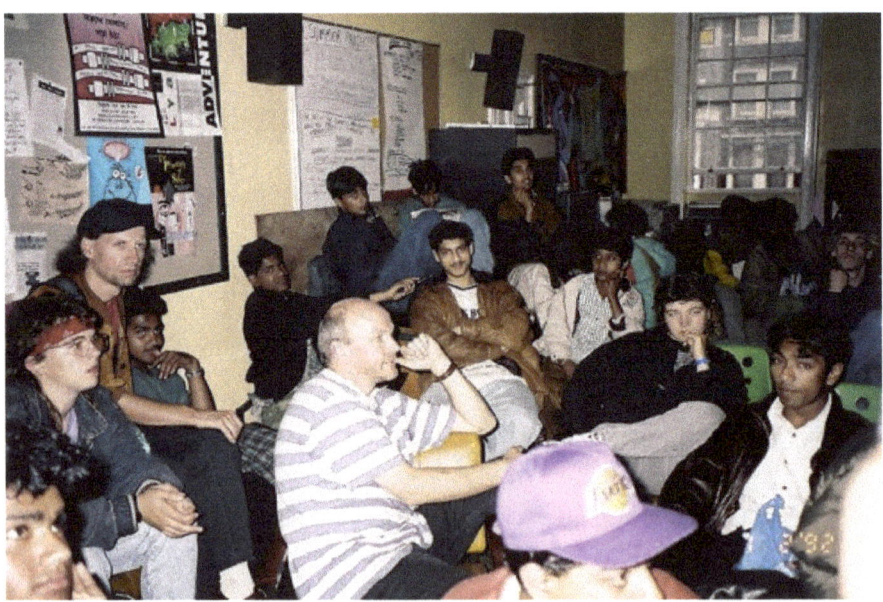

East End Photos, Through Mayar's Eyes : Voluntary Sector 1992-1993

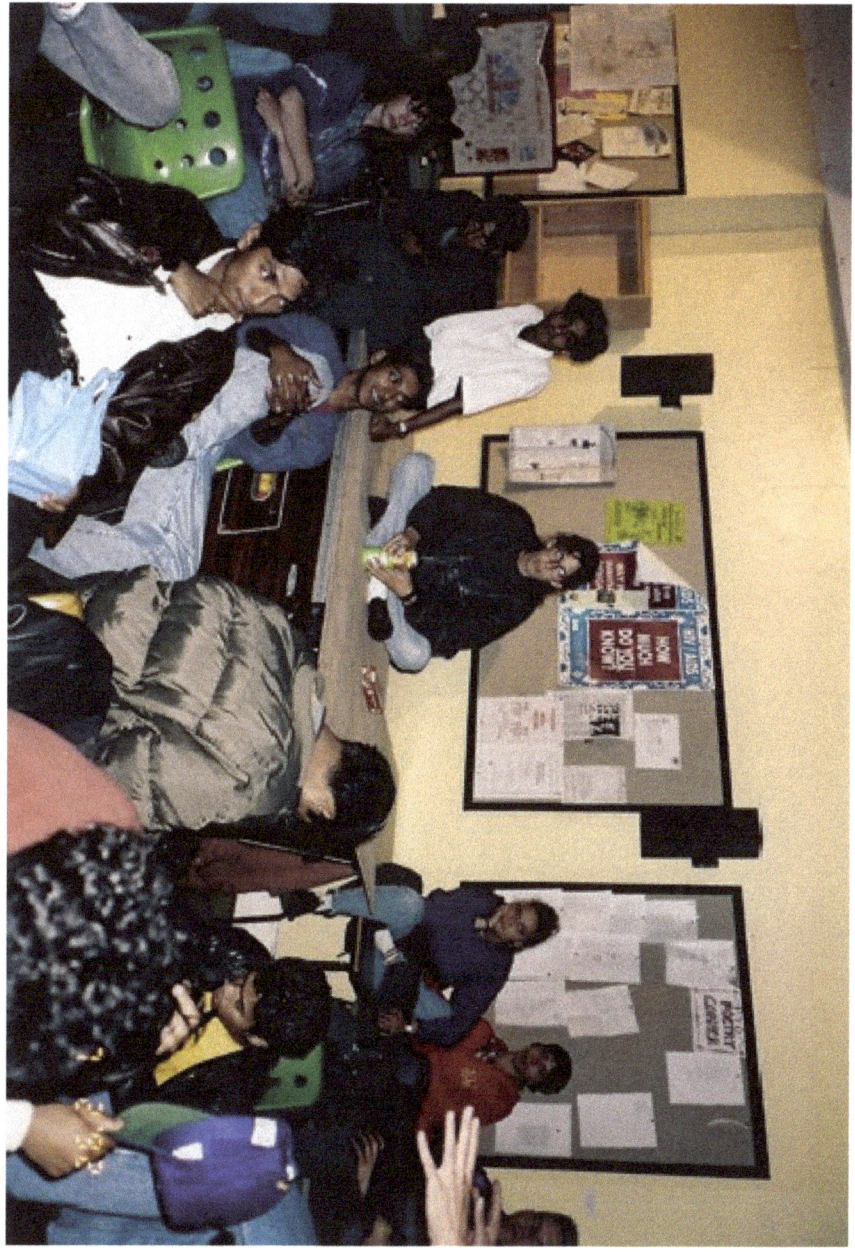

7.3.91992 - Hoxton Venue

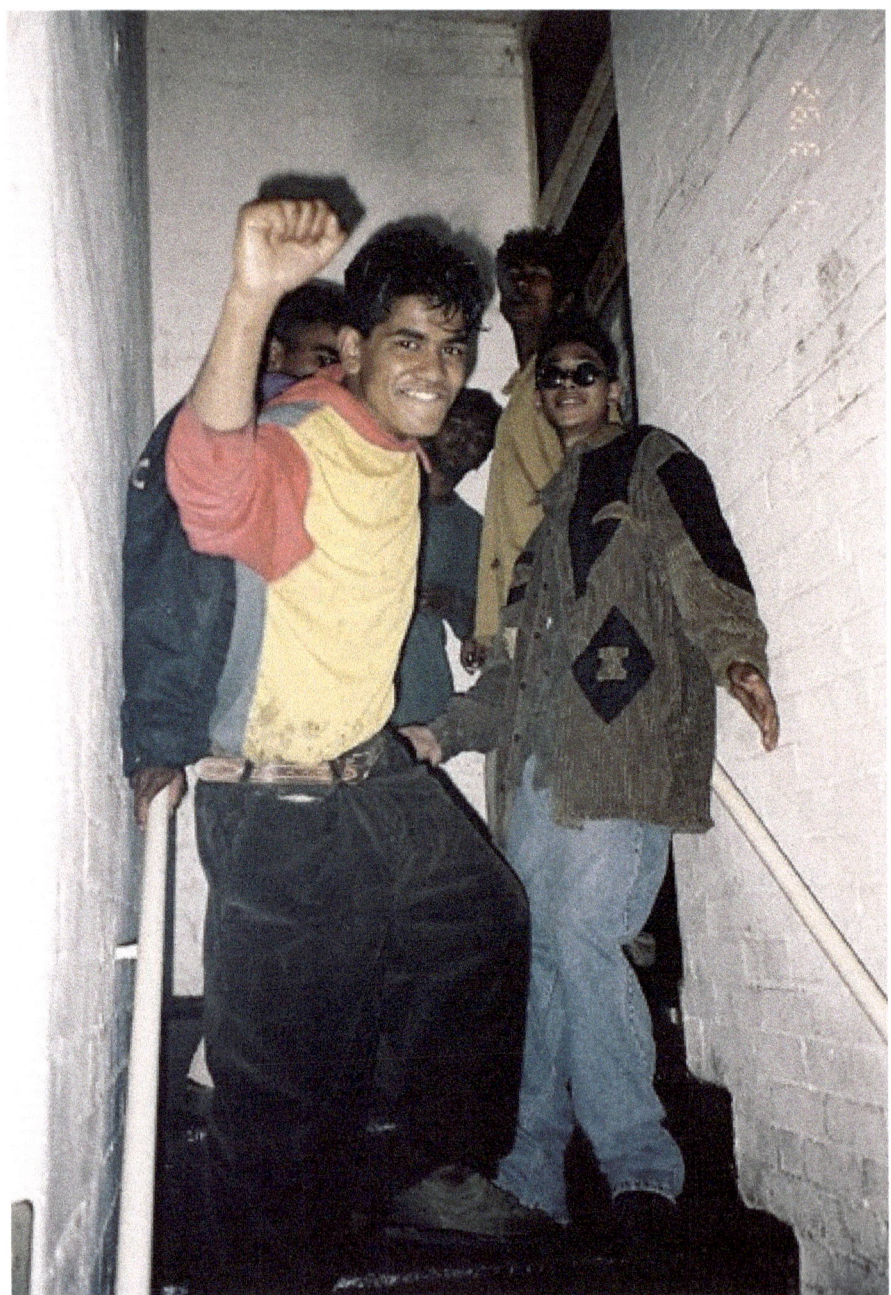

East End Photos, Through Mayar's Eyes : Voluntary Sector 1992-1993

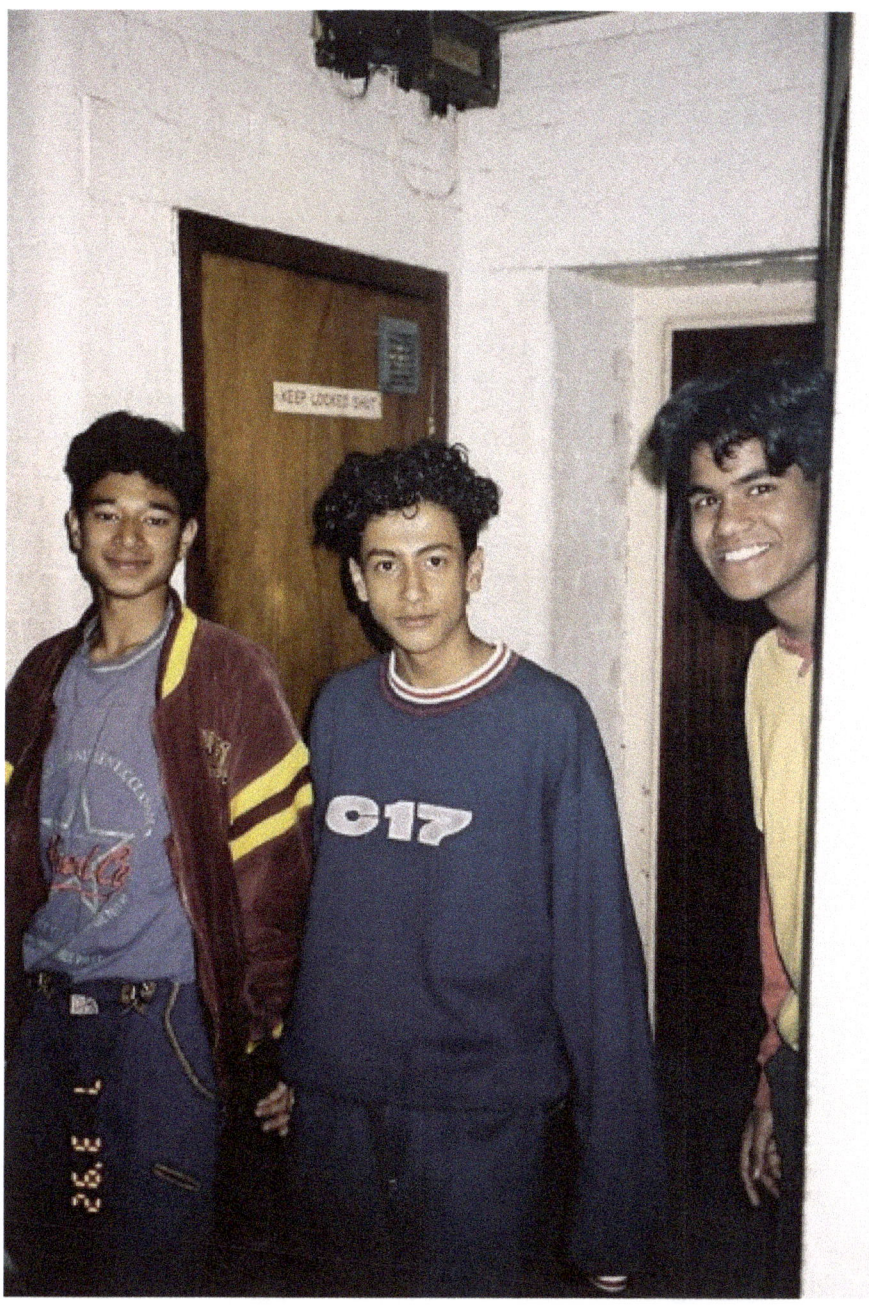

Billy Boy

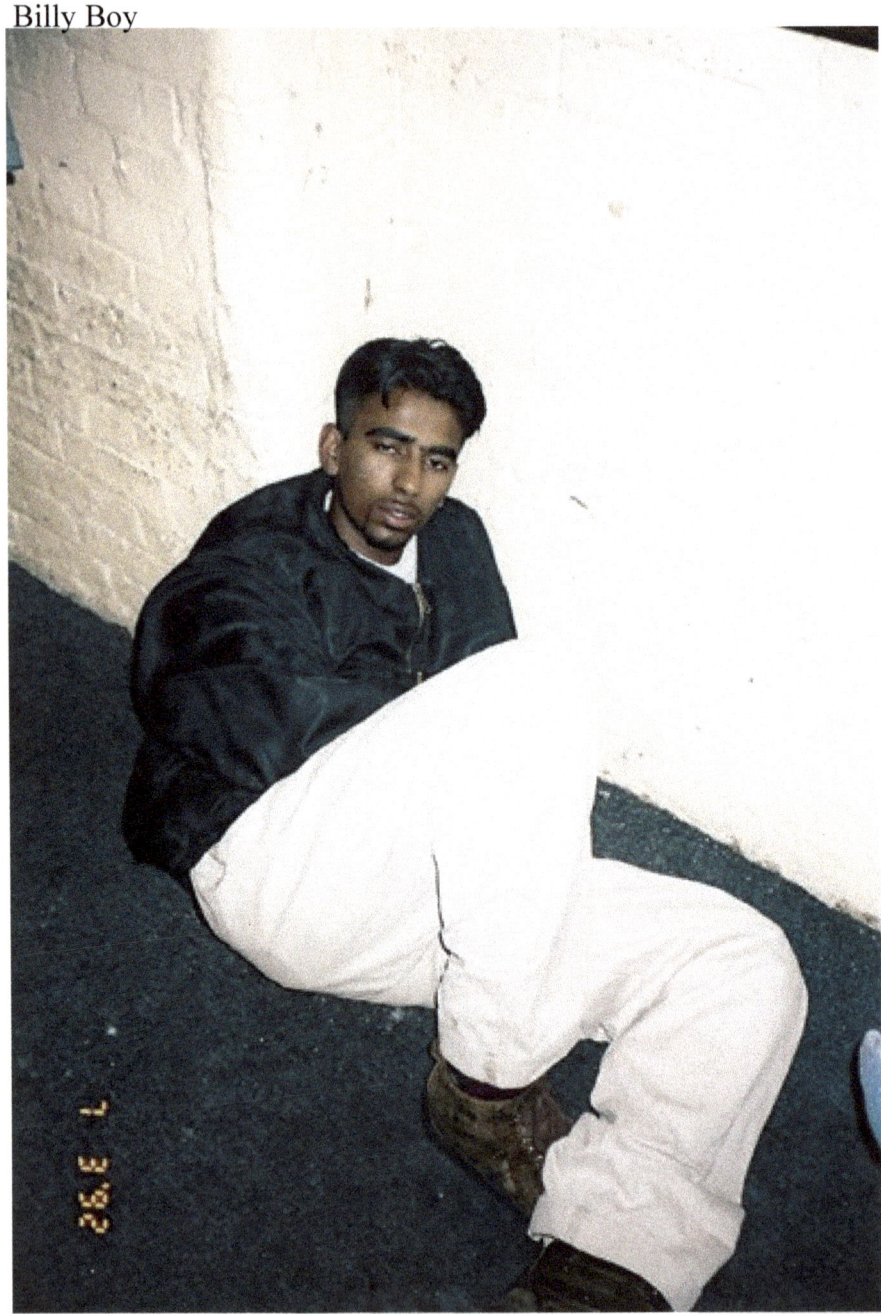

Light weight, dizzy whizzy

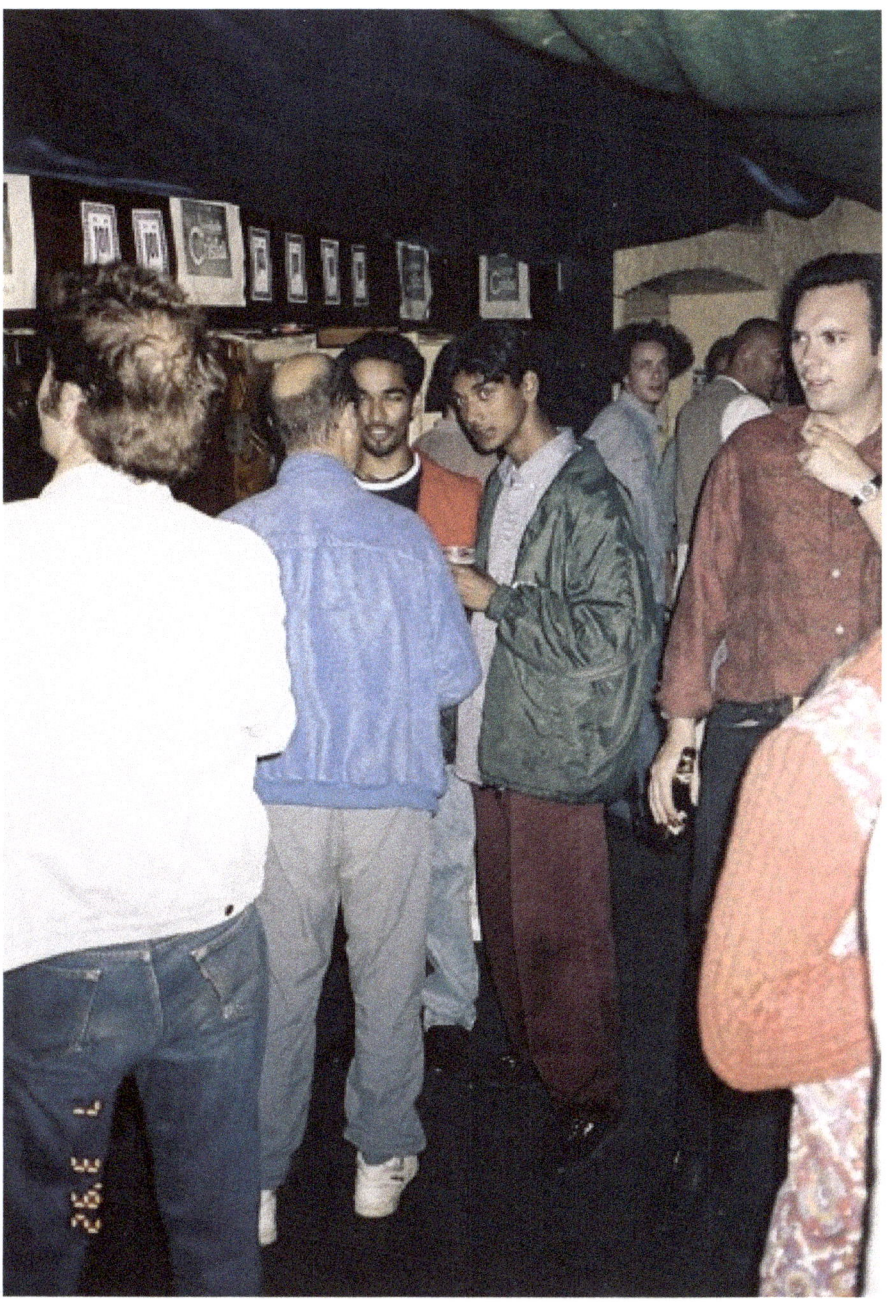
David Hollowing chatting with the boys.

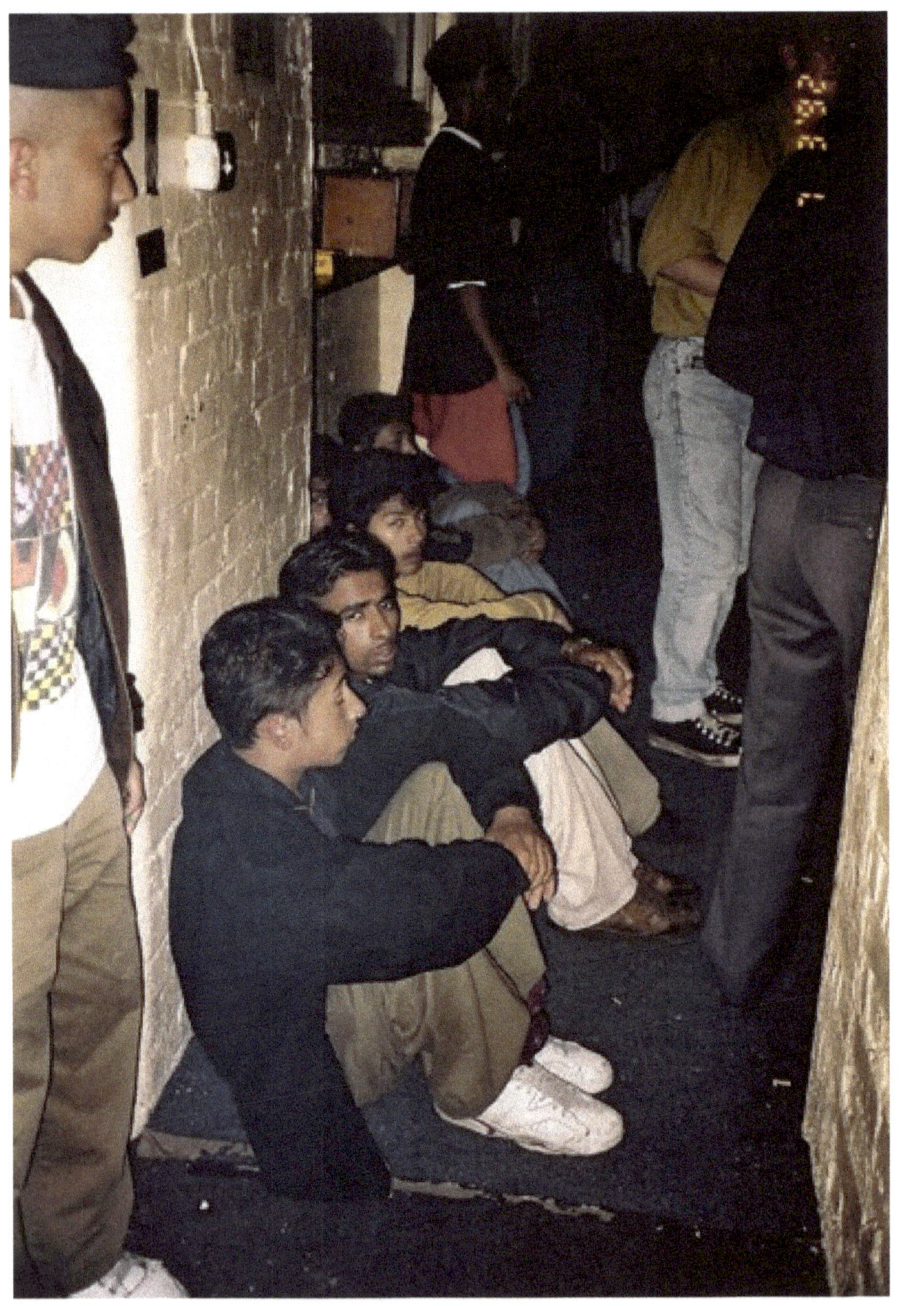

Check out the rave scene!!! Too knackered…

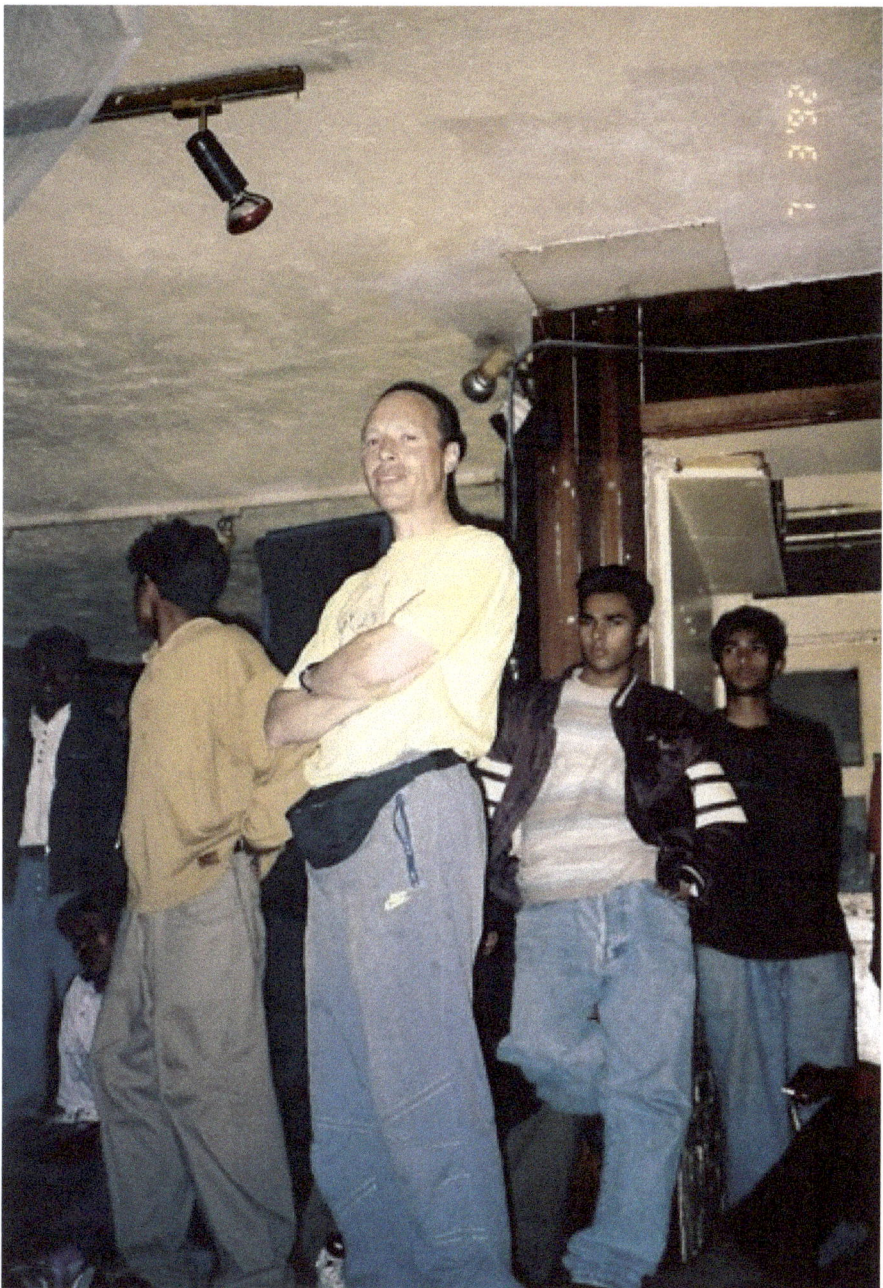

David Holloway, Gessi, Mo Magic and the rave scene. Rohim and Muktar Ahmed in the scene.

August Party in Woodseer Youth Centre 21.8.1992

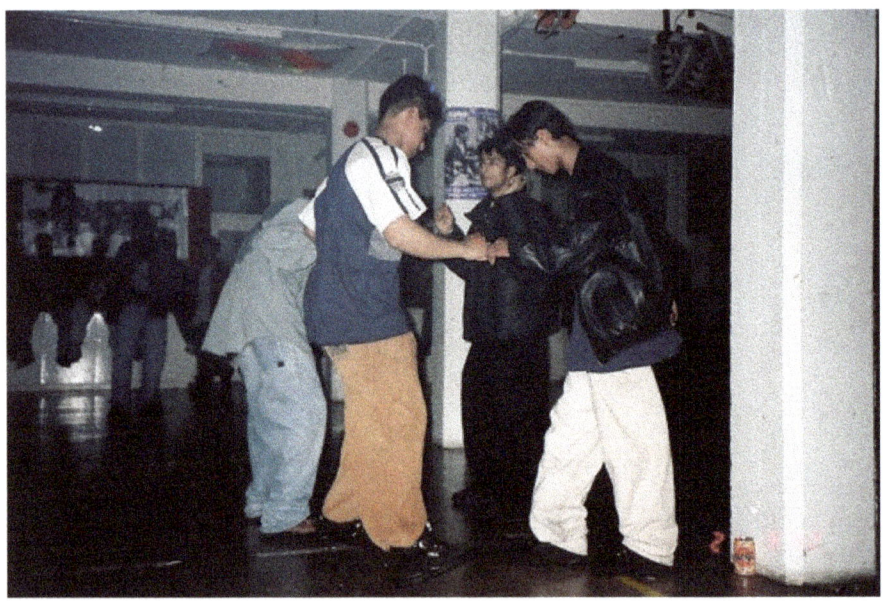

Chilling while music was raving.

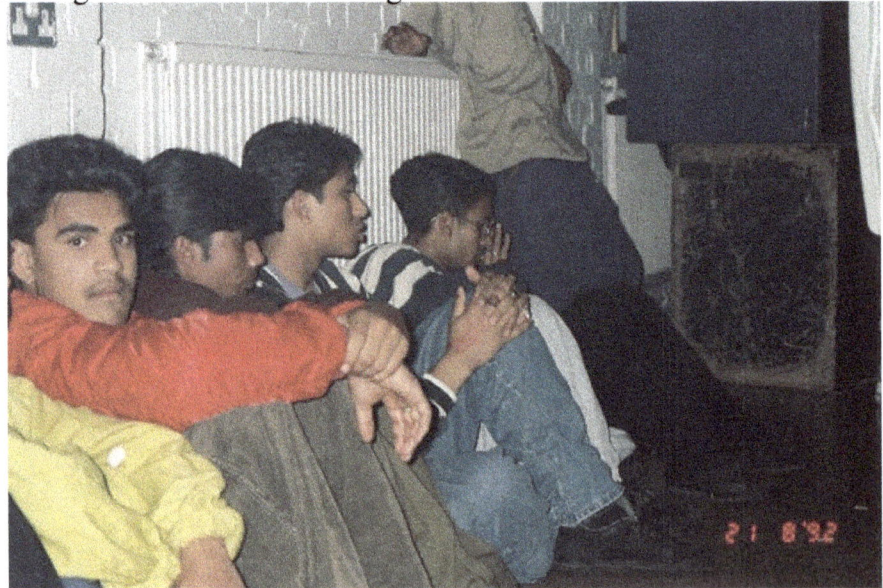

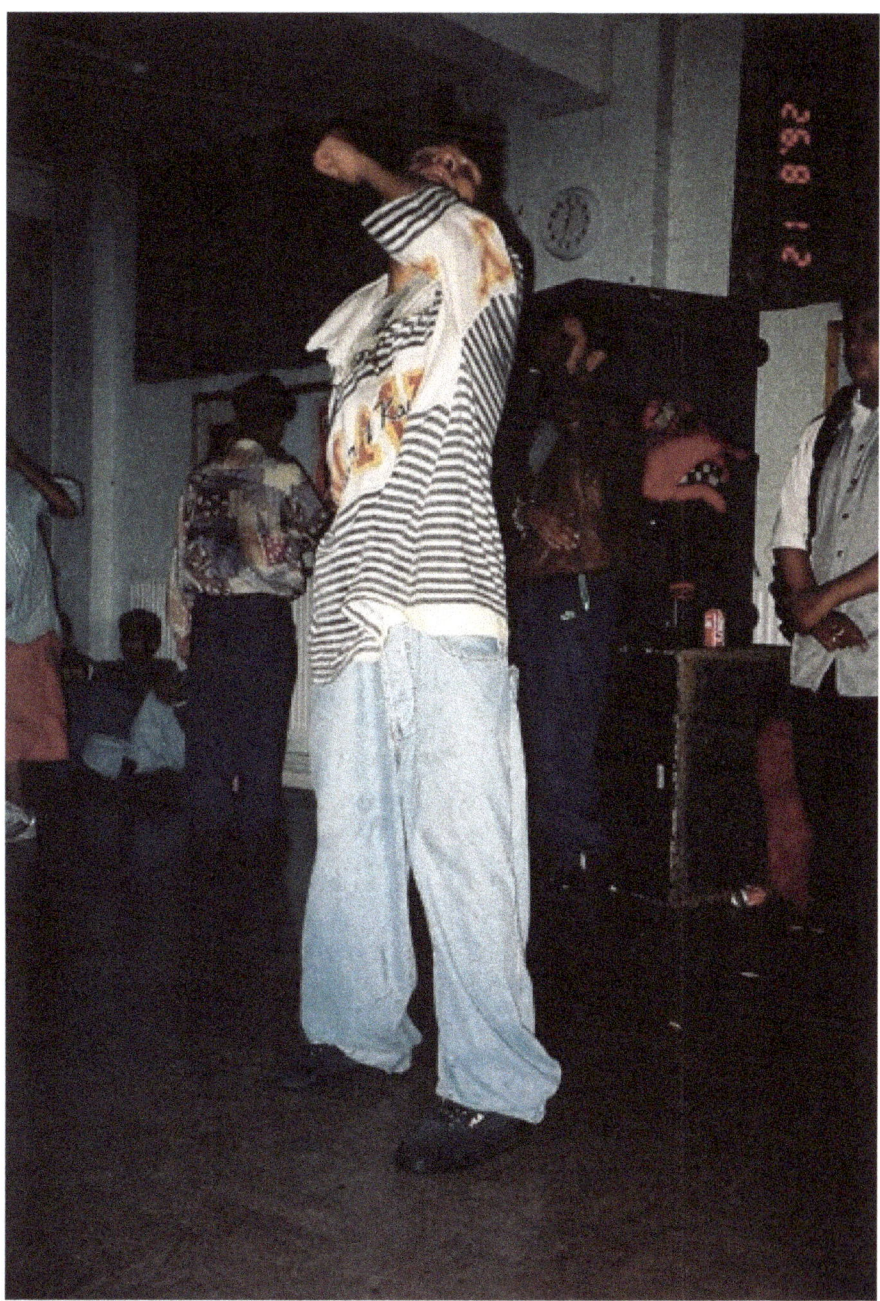

Dance mania!

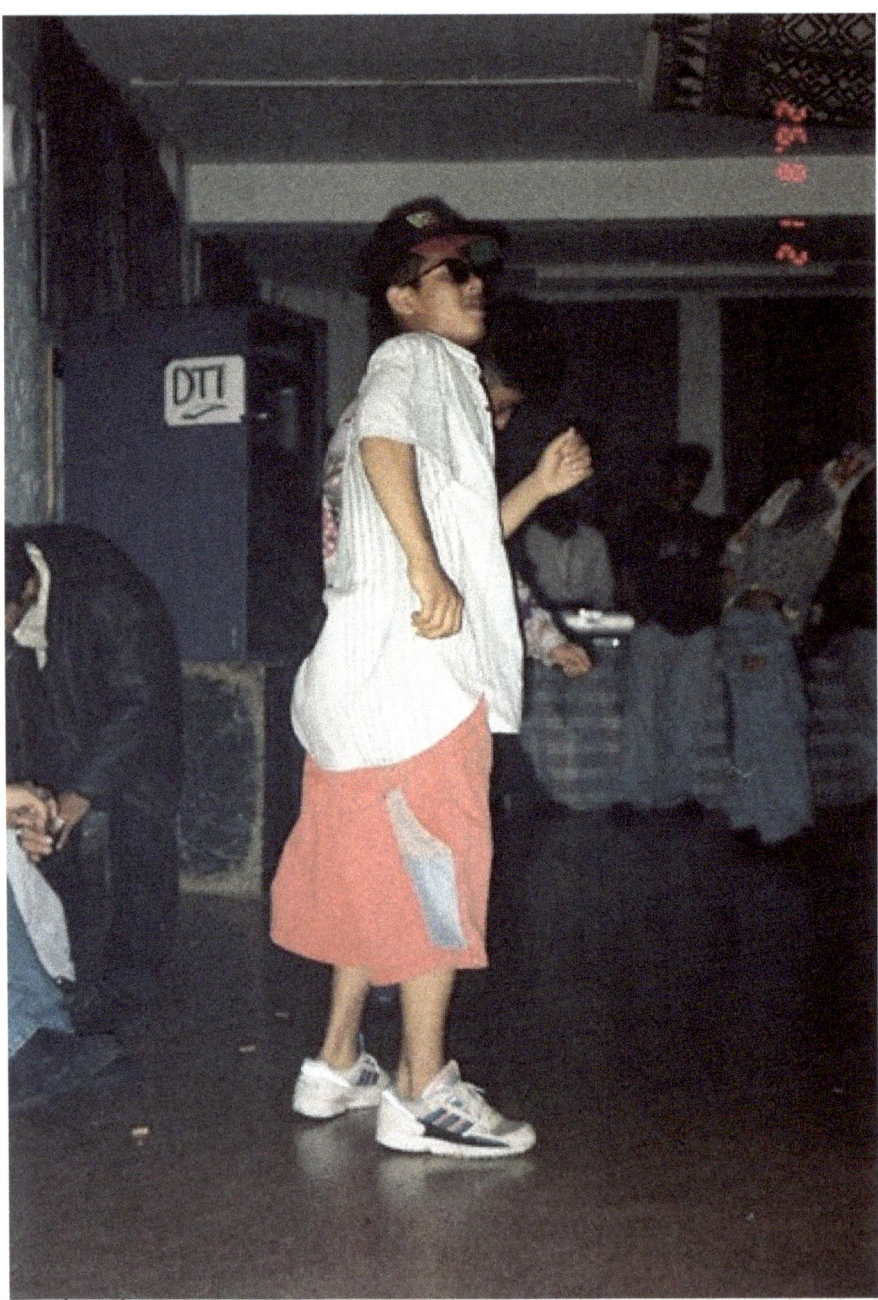

Busting those moves!

Summer University @ Tower Hamlets College

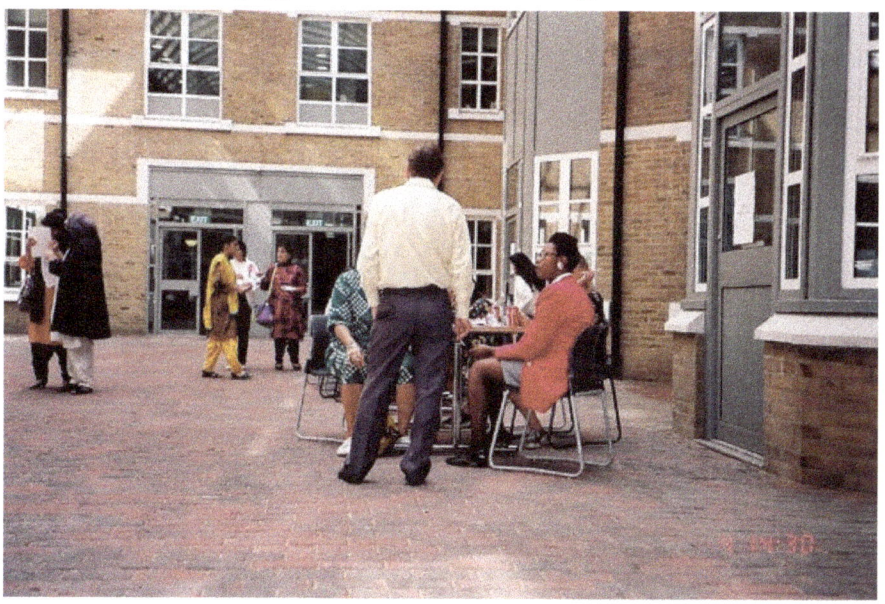

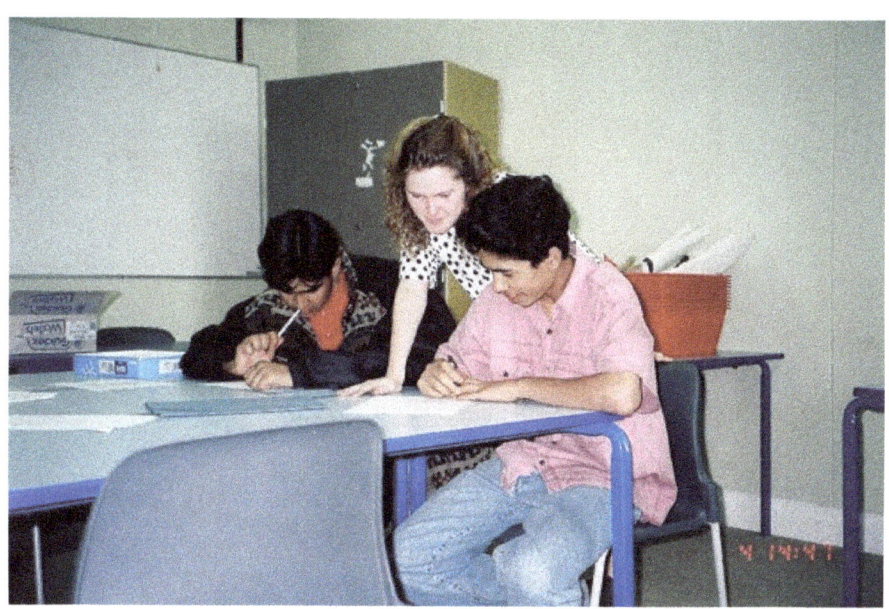

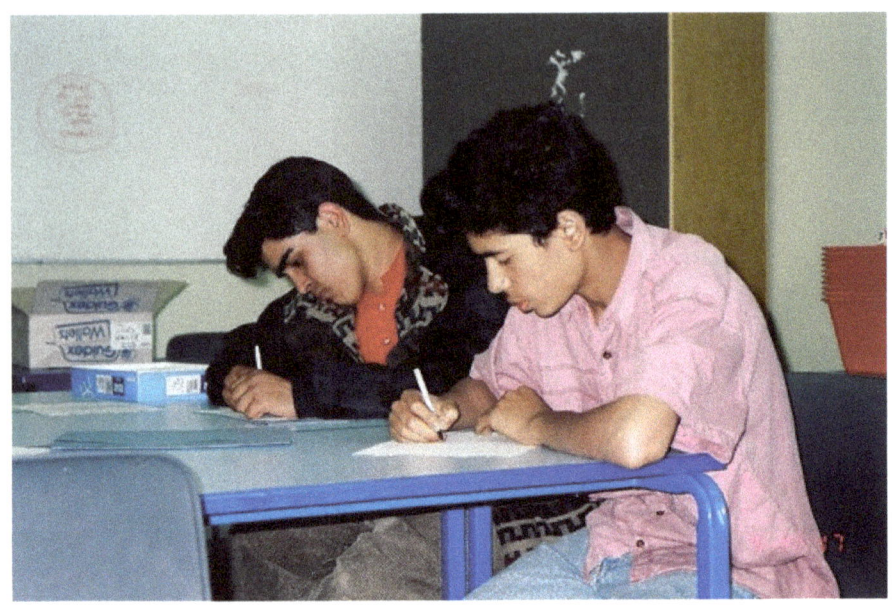

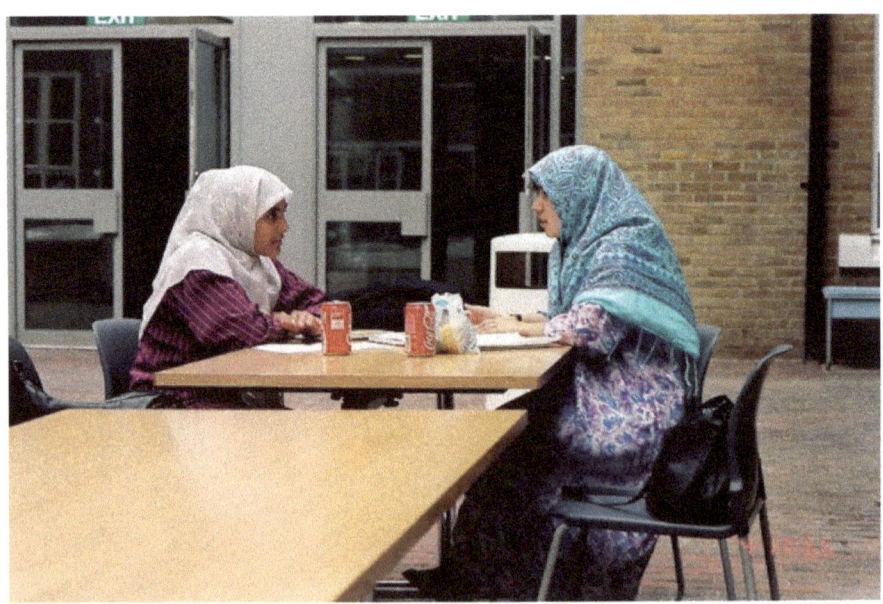

East End Photos, Through Mayar's Eyes : Voluntary Sector 1992-1993

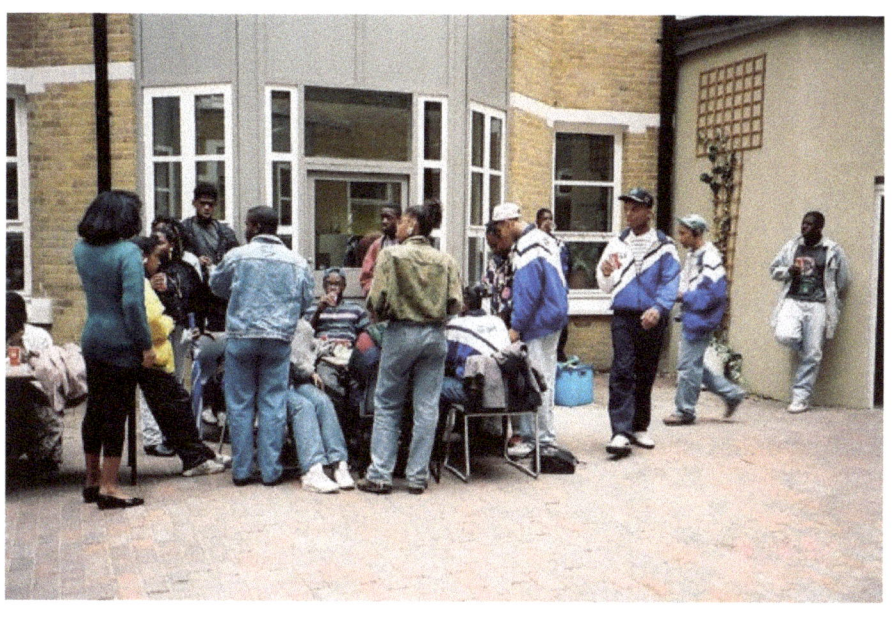

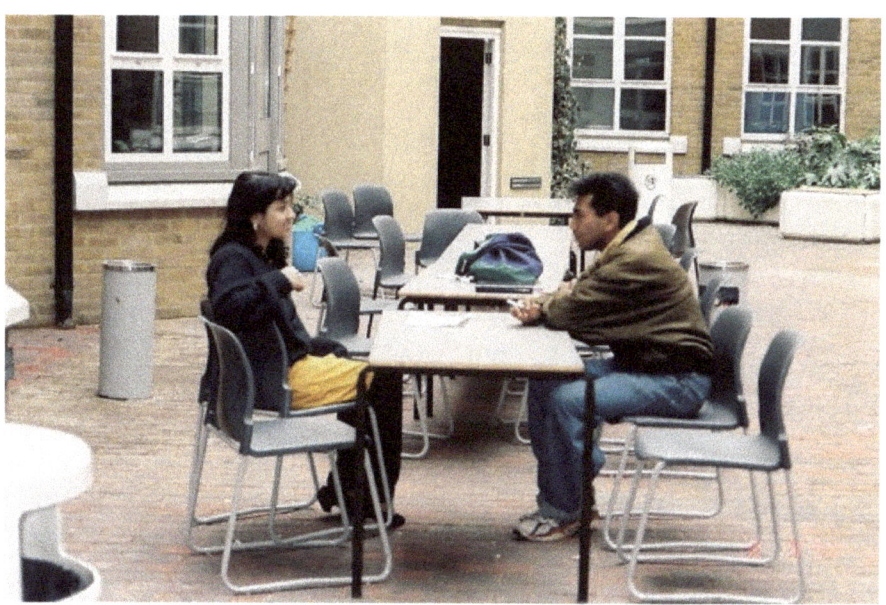

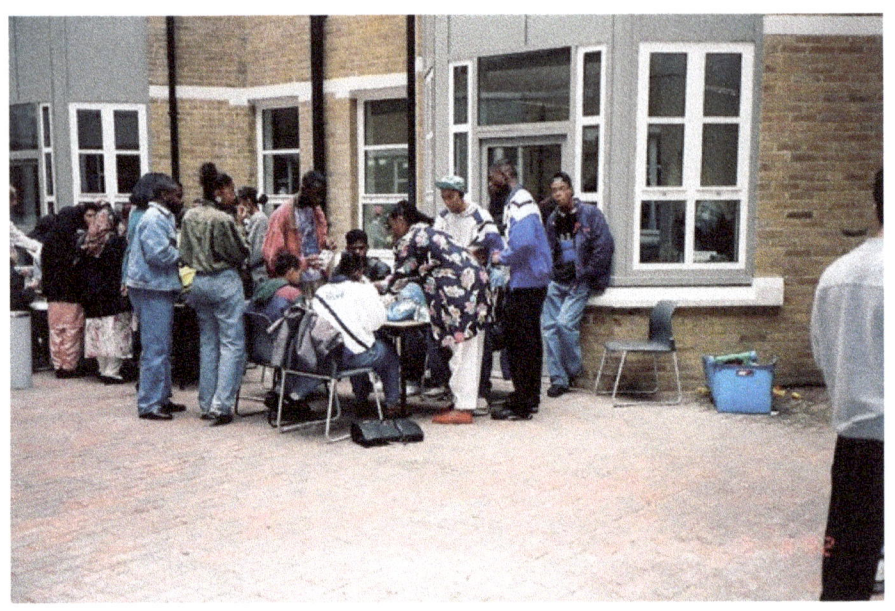

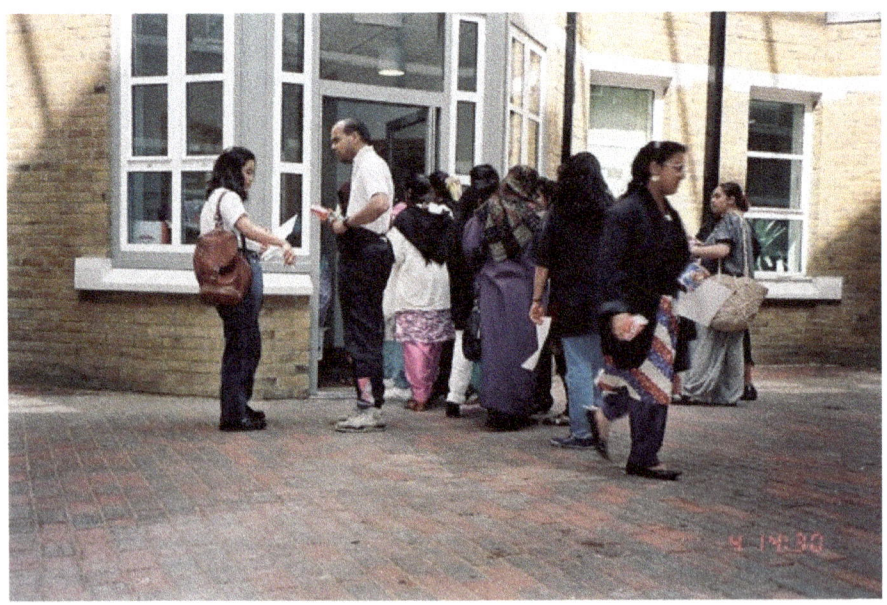

East End Photos, Through Mayar's Eyes : Voluntary Sector 1992-1993

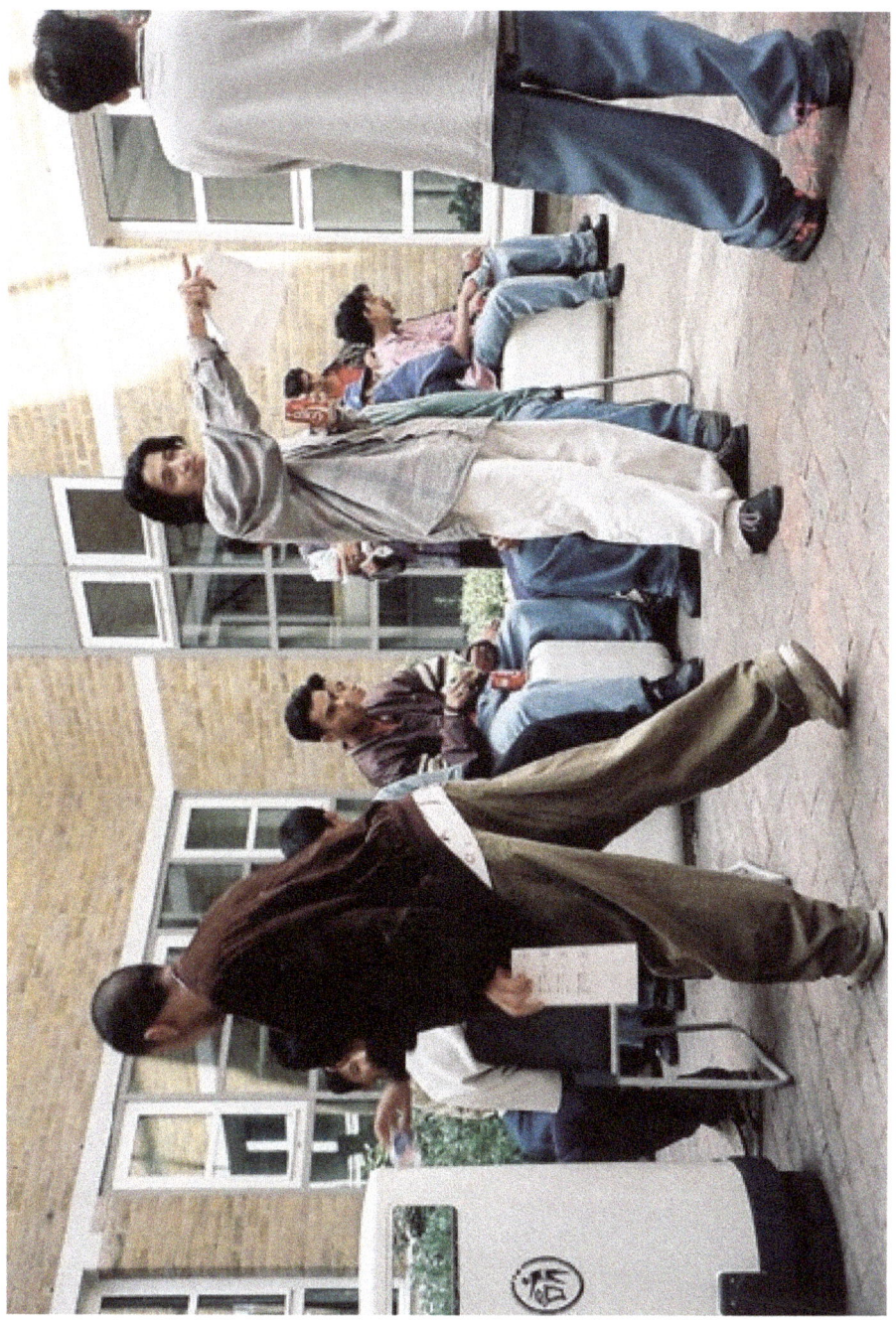

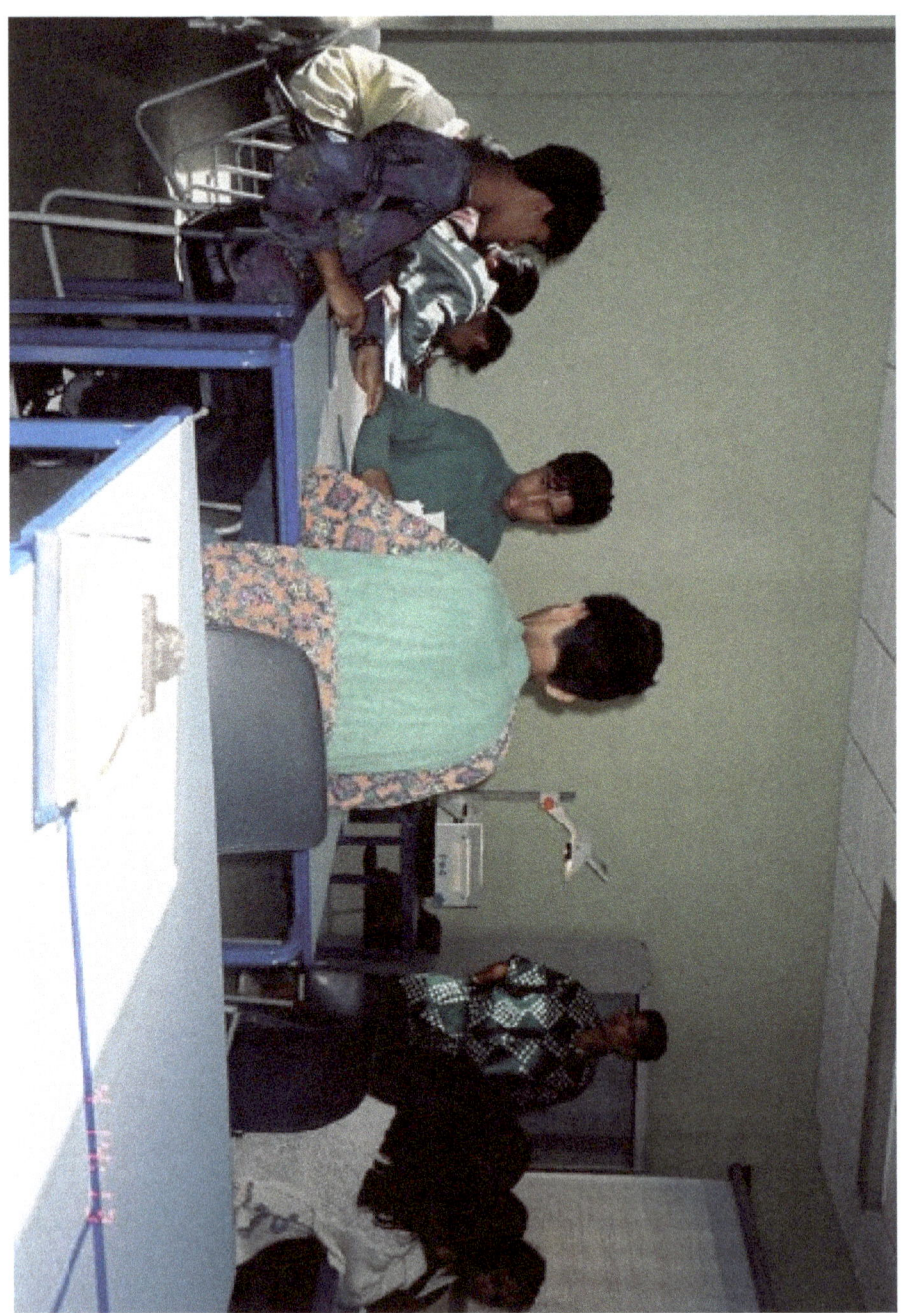

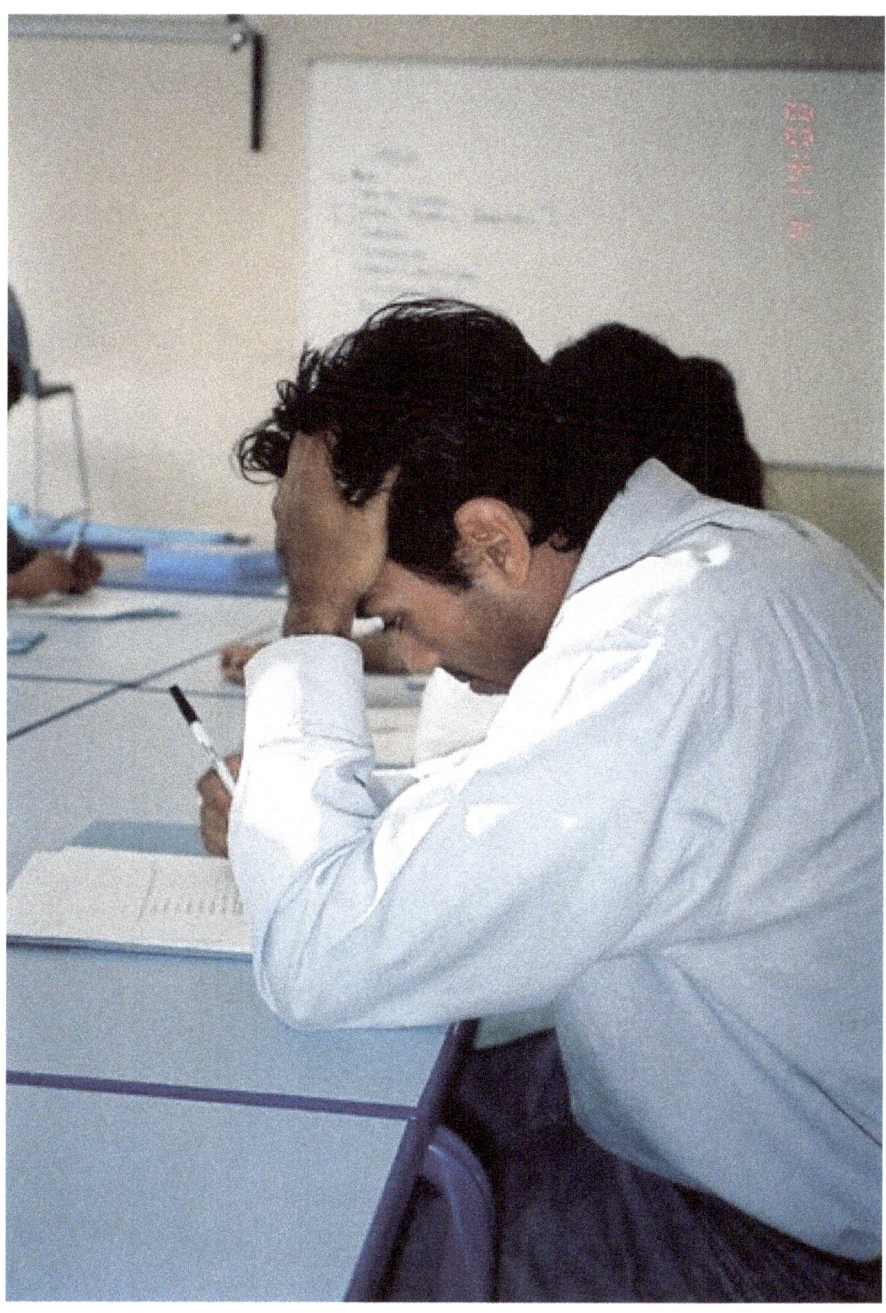

Zorrul hard at work!

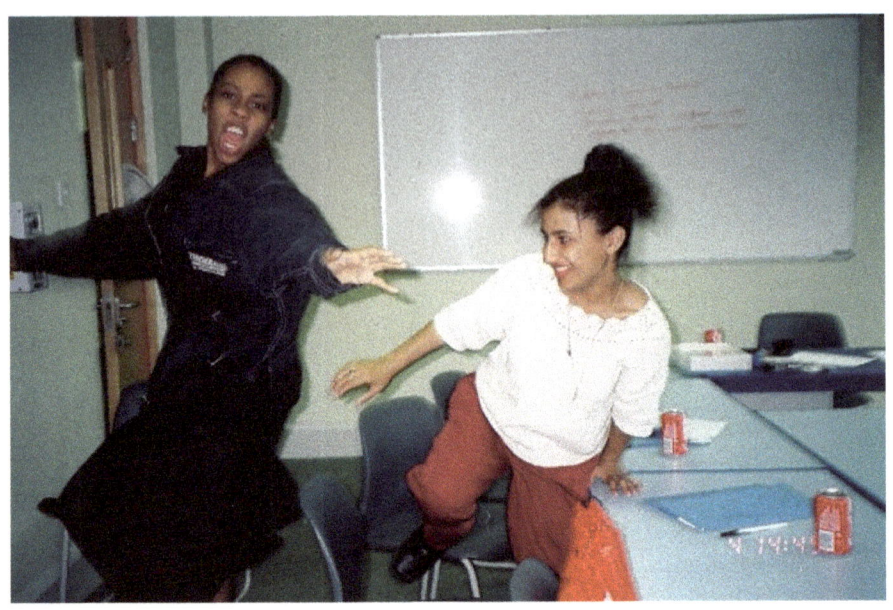

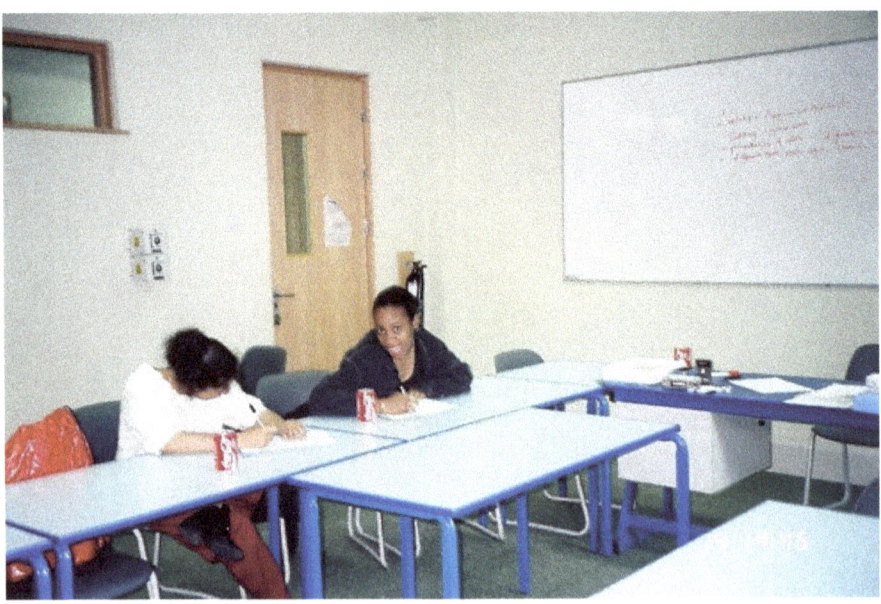

East End Photos, Through Mayar's Eyes : Voluntary Sector 1992-1993

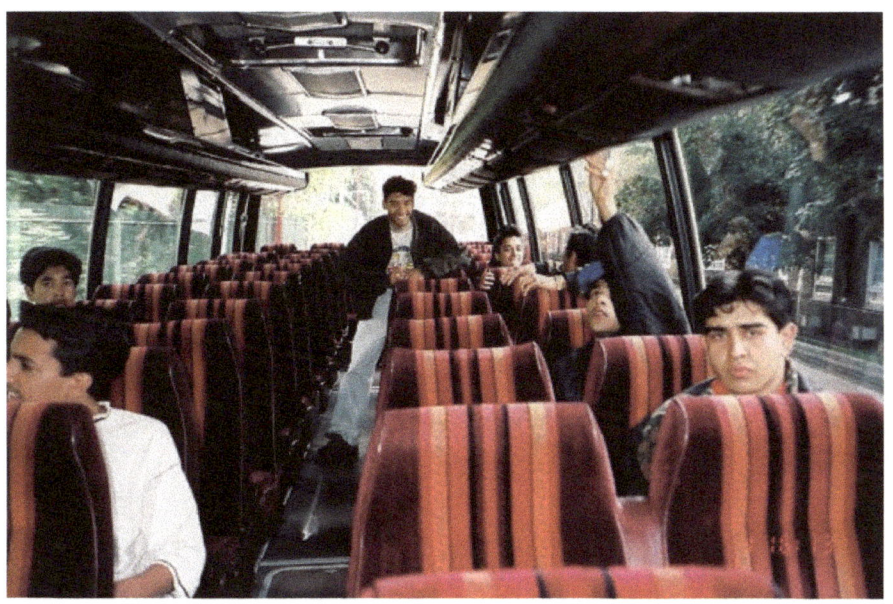

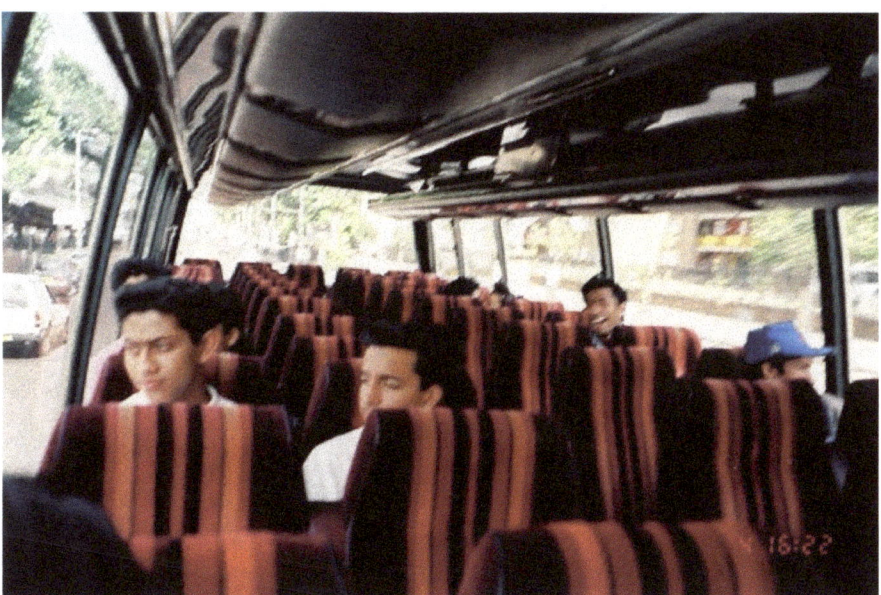

Transporting the youth to Summer University, aka Tower Hamlets College

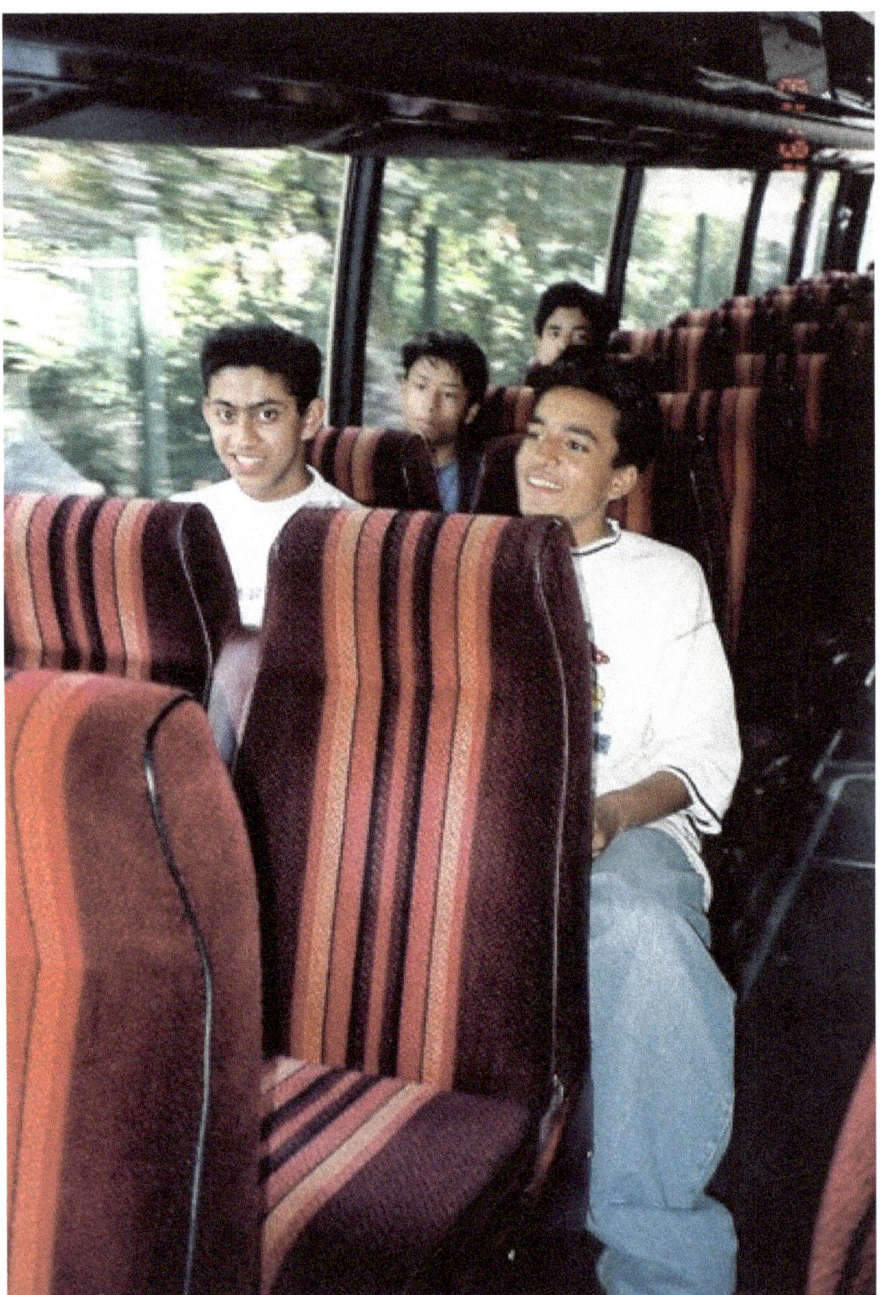

Aliur, did you know you would become a Tea master 25 years from now?

East End Photos, Through Mayar's Eyes : Voluntary Sector 1992-1993

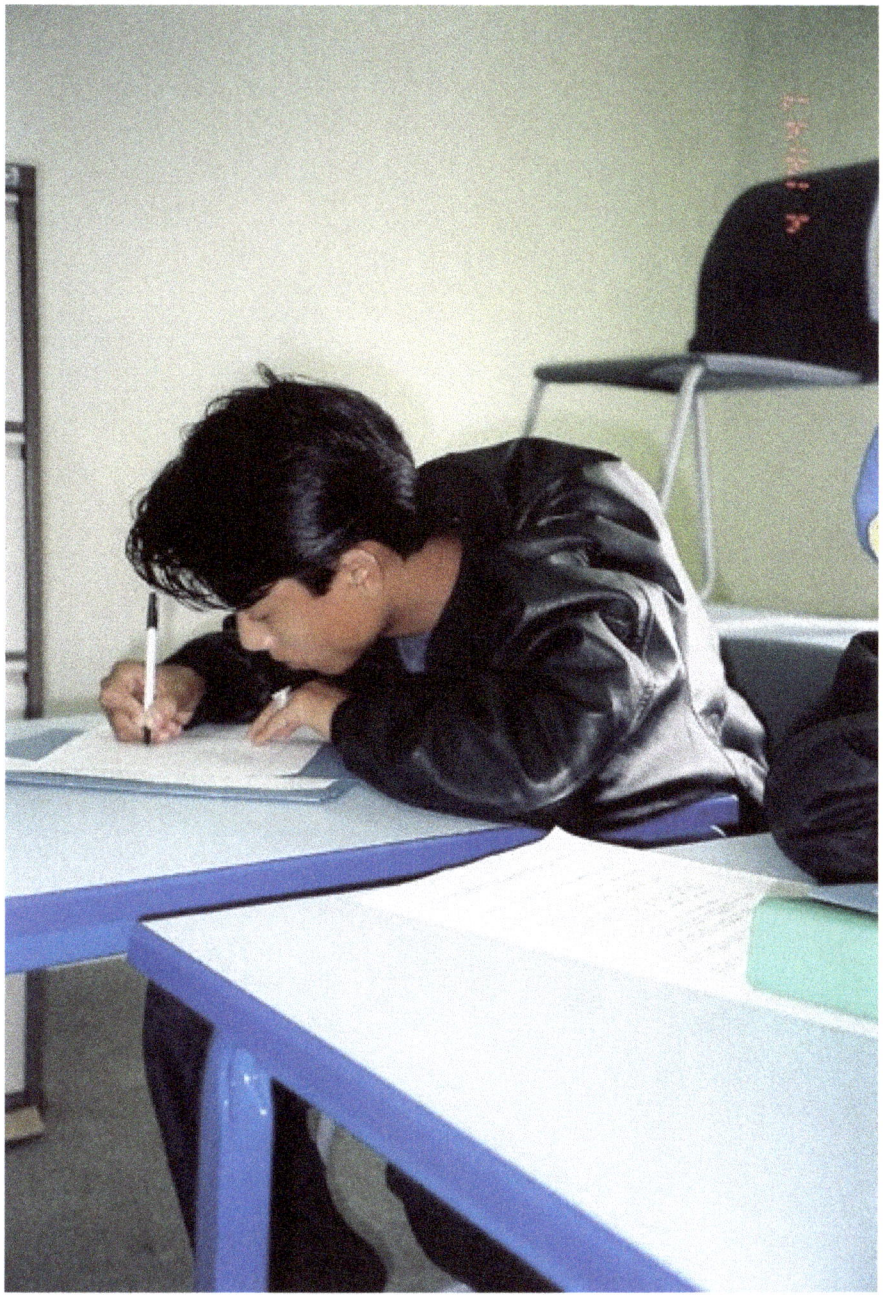

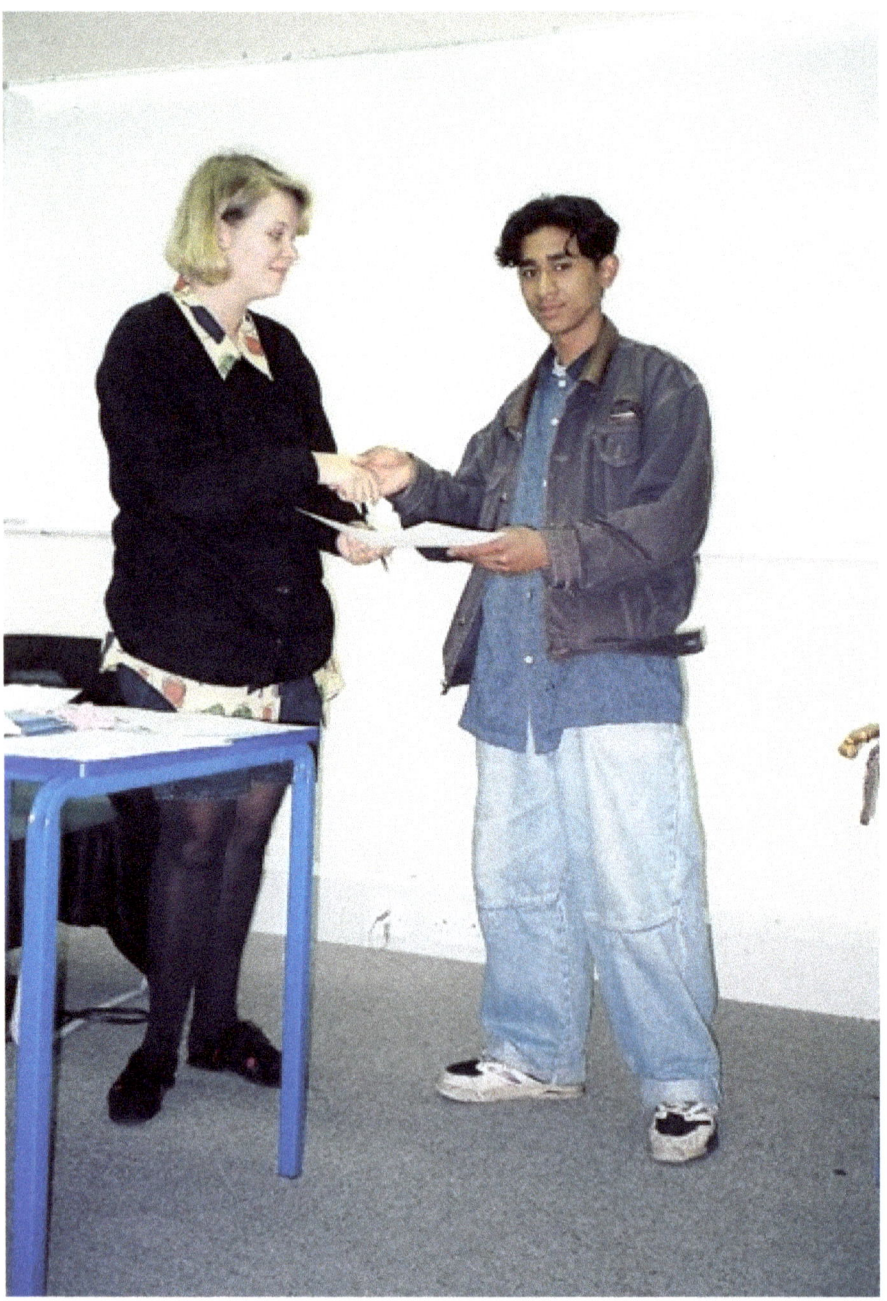

Shamim of Shoreditch, Boundary estate, getting his certificate,

Collingwood Estate

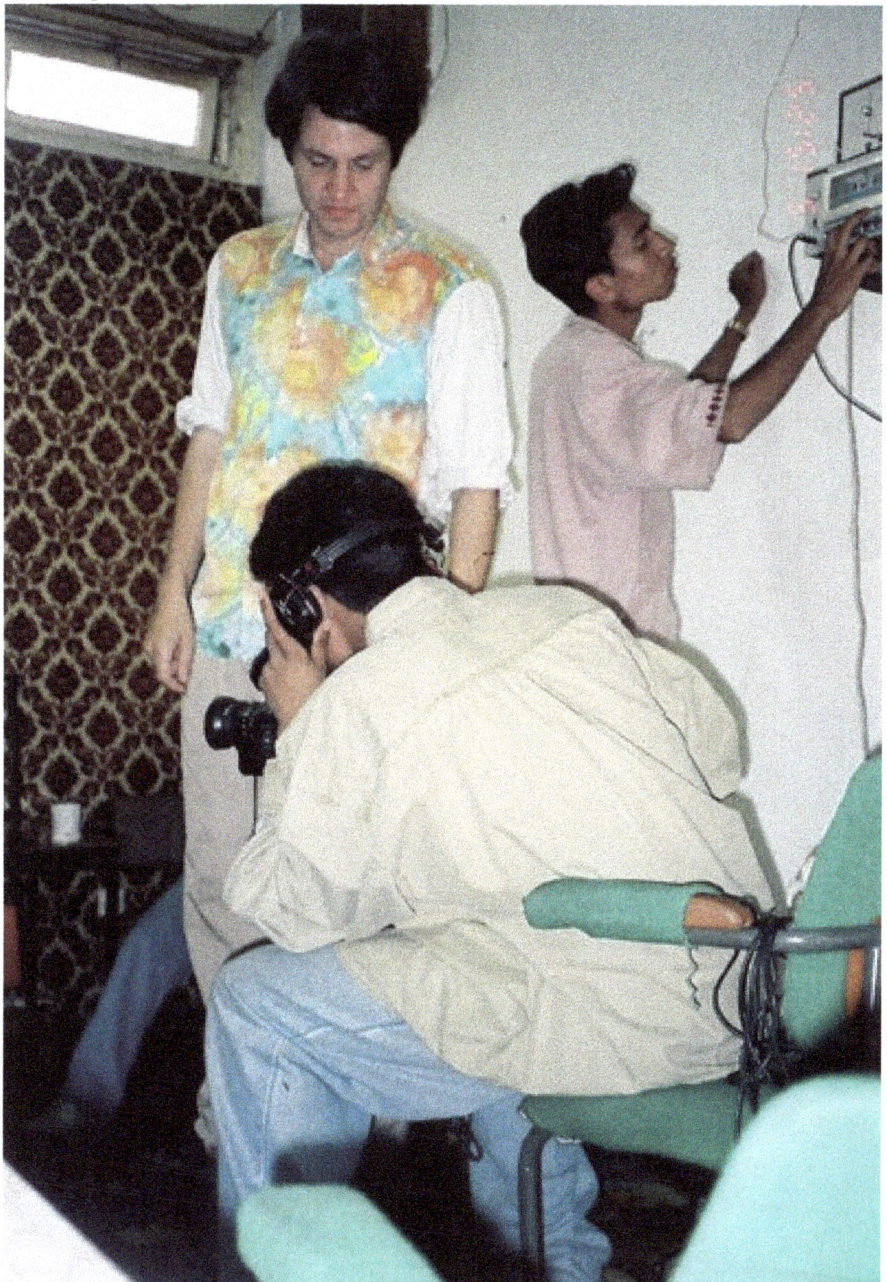

ADI Running Filming workshop in Collingwood Estate TA Hall

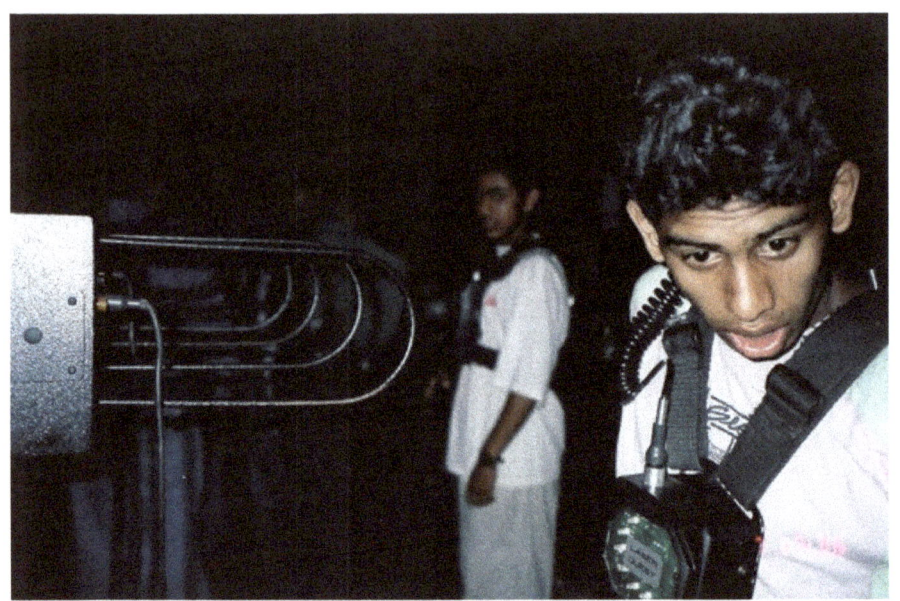

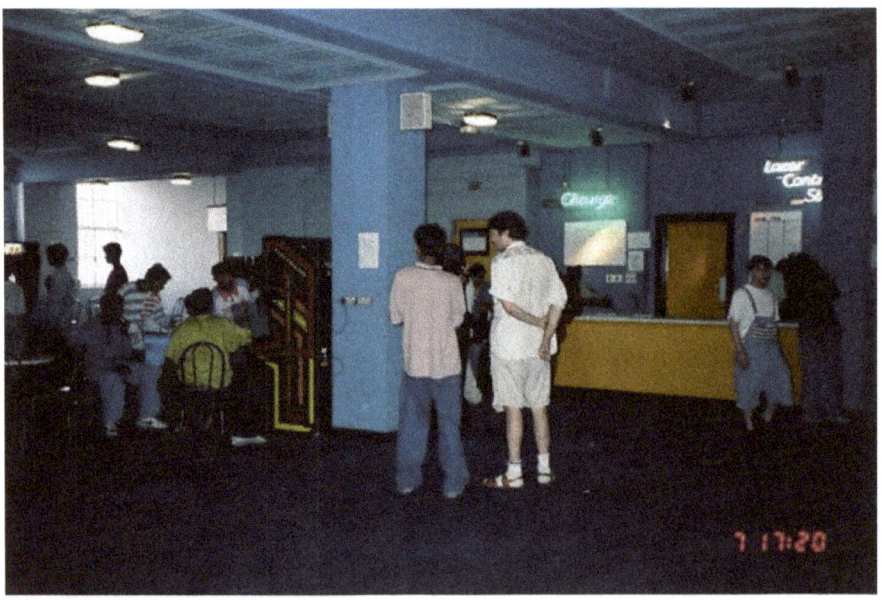

East London Line

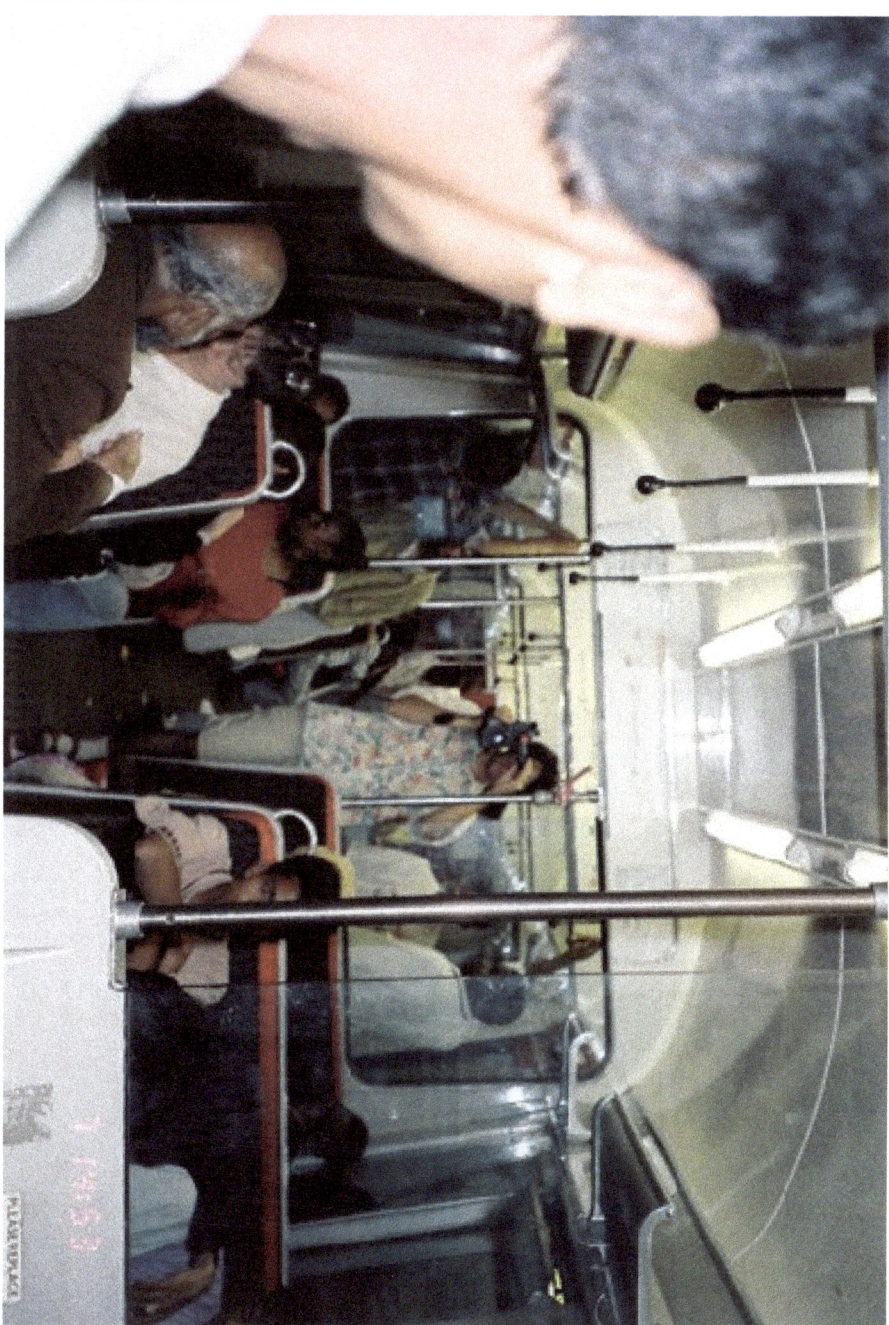

Filming on the underground tube rail.

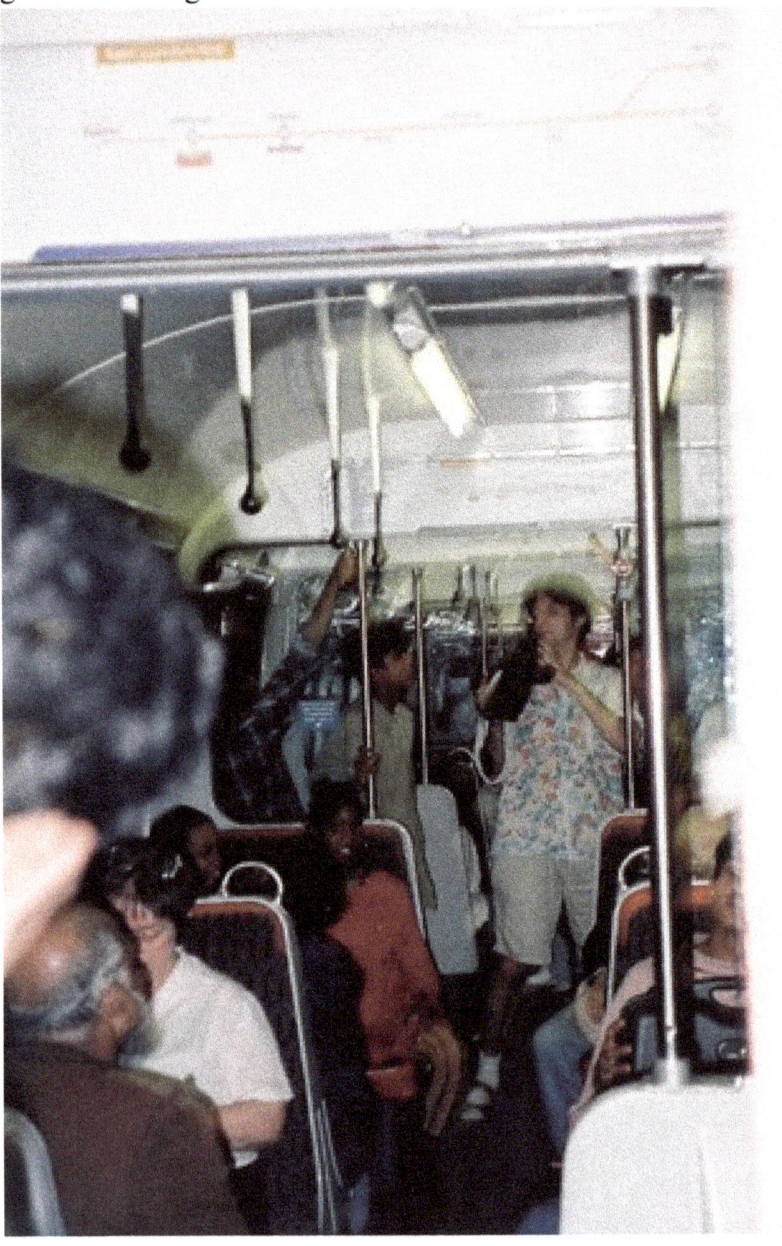

23.12.1992 Christmass Party!! at PYO

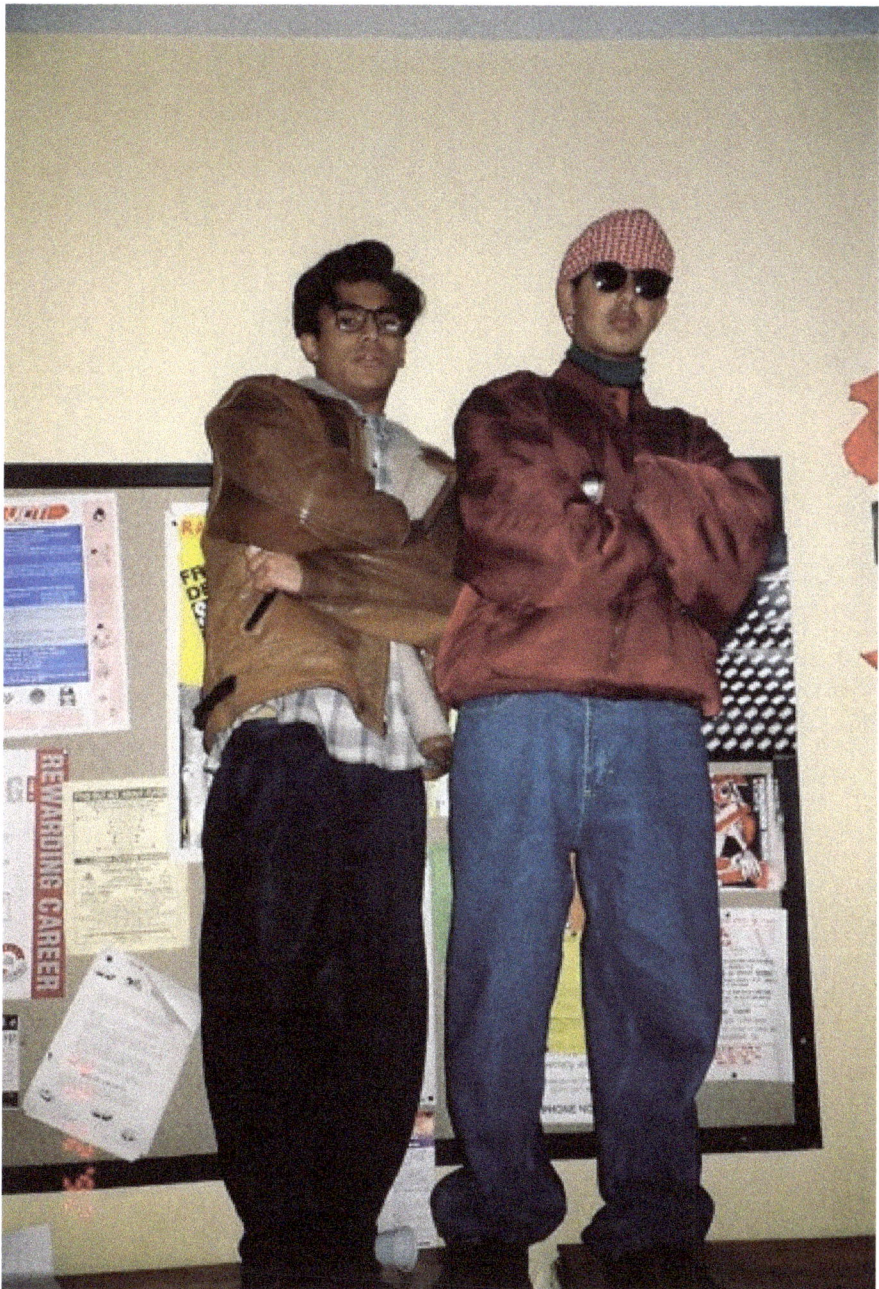

Hoodzmanz in da house!!

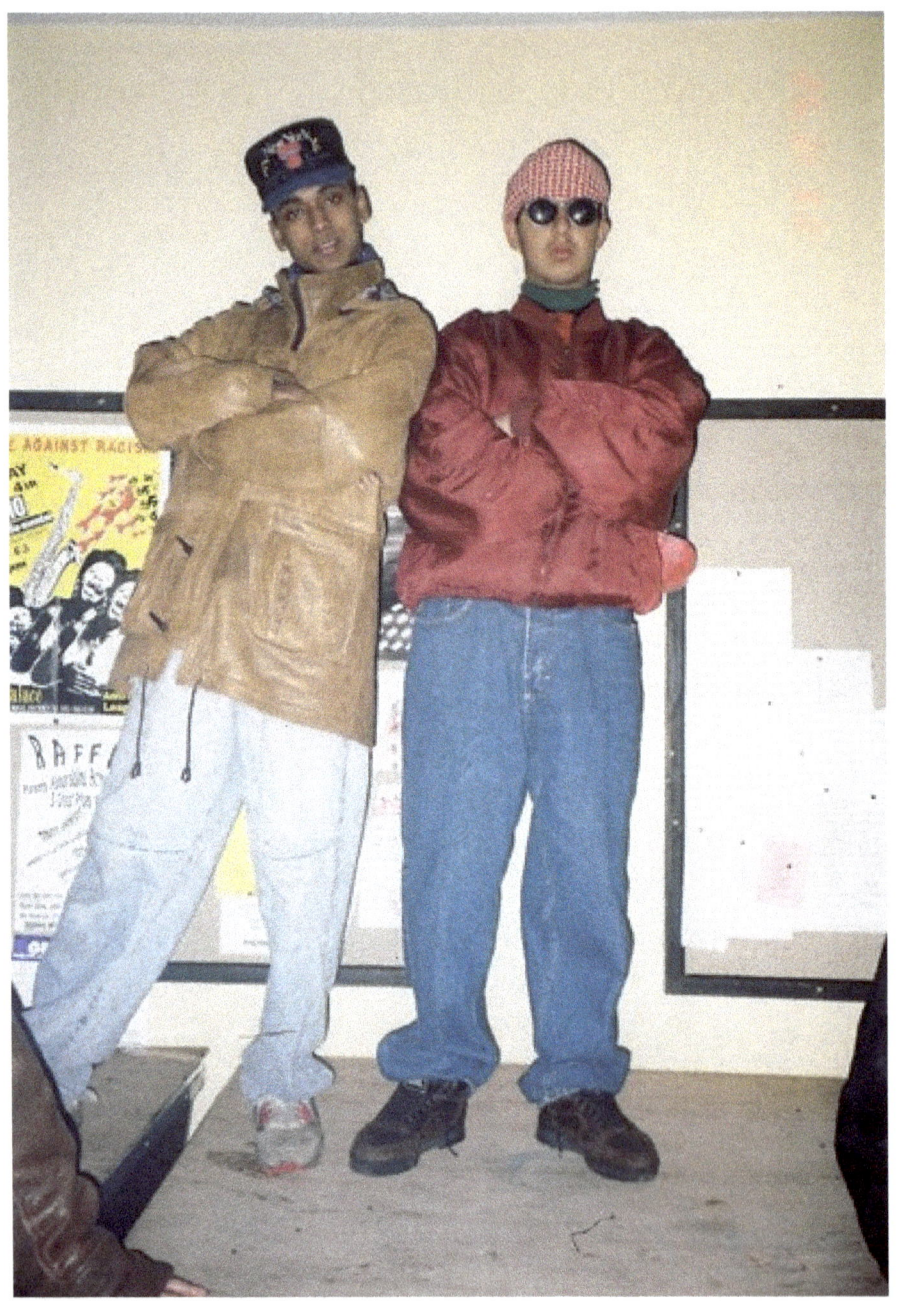

East End Photos, Through Mayar's Eyes : Voluntary Sector 1992-1993

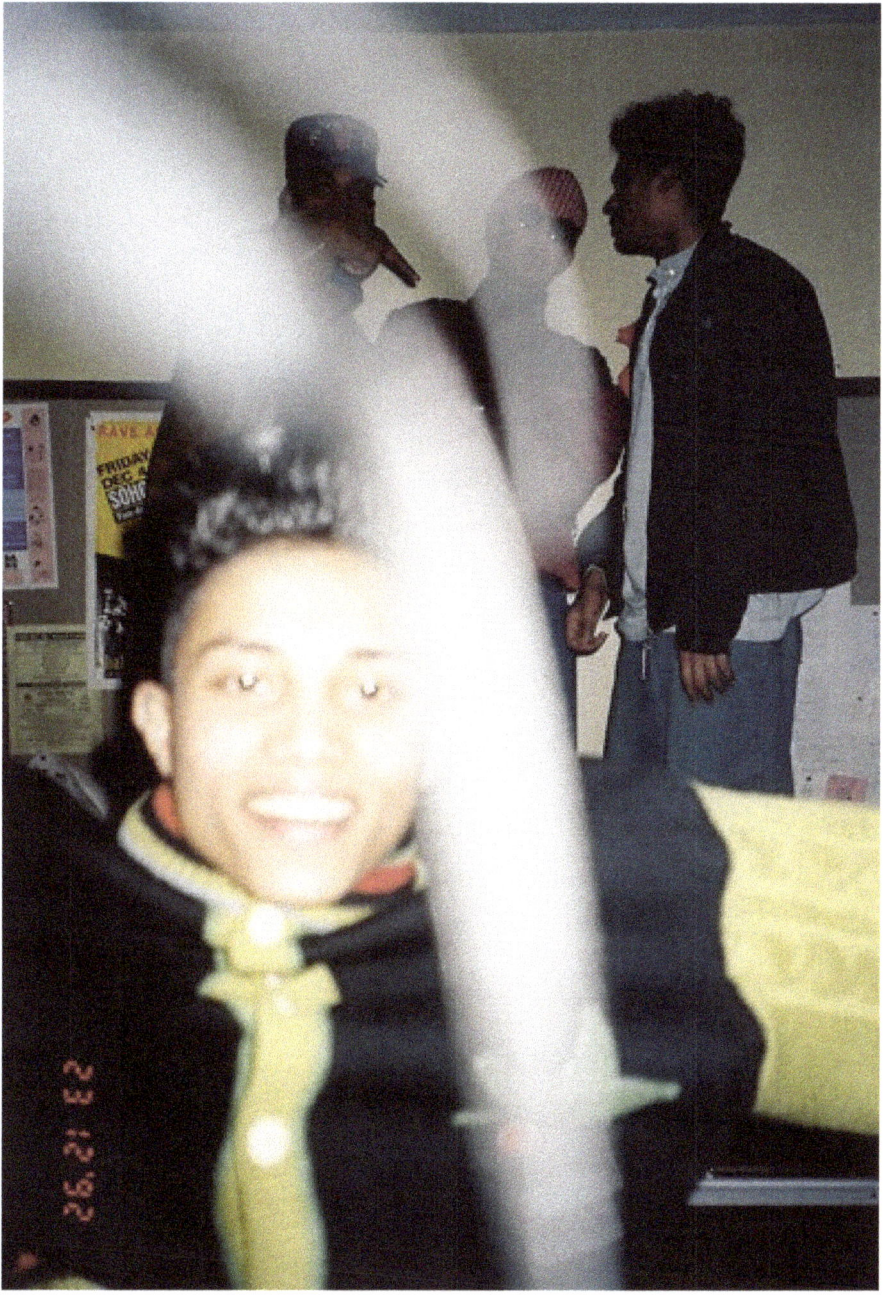

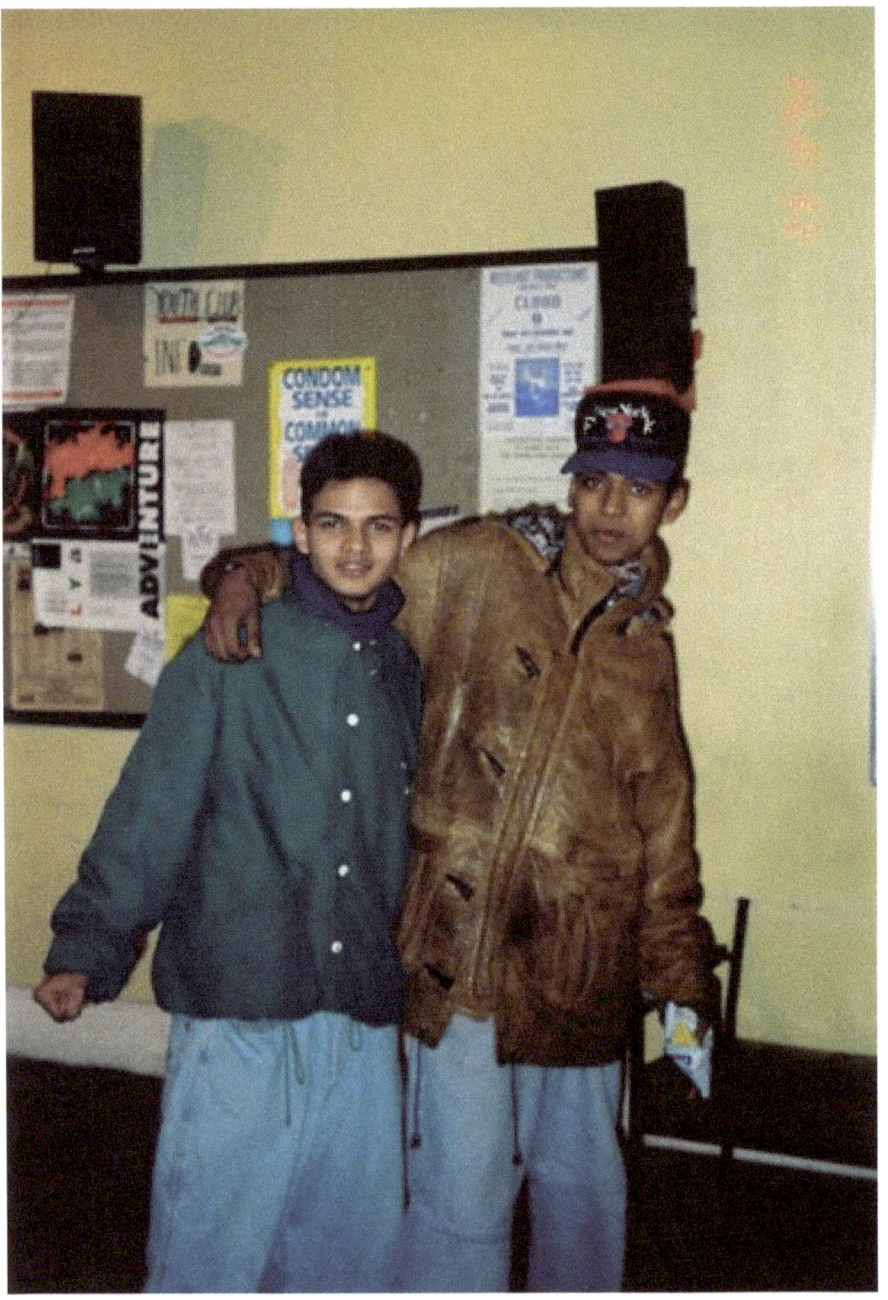

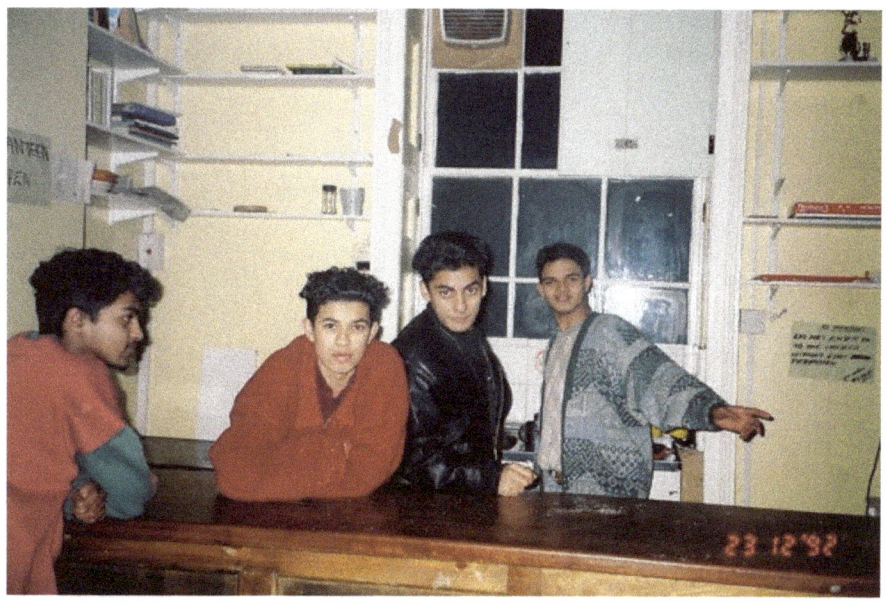

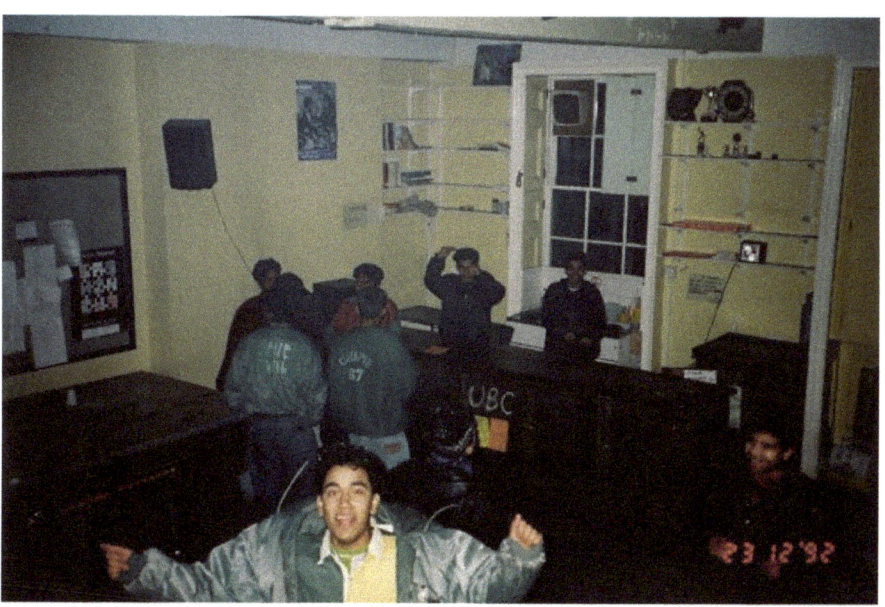

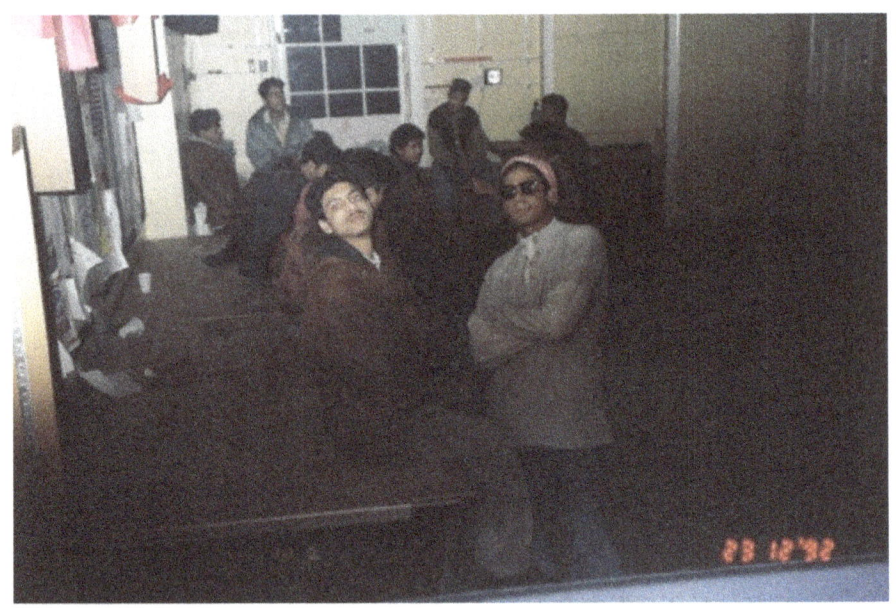

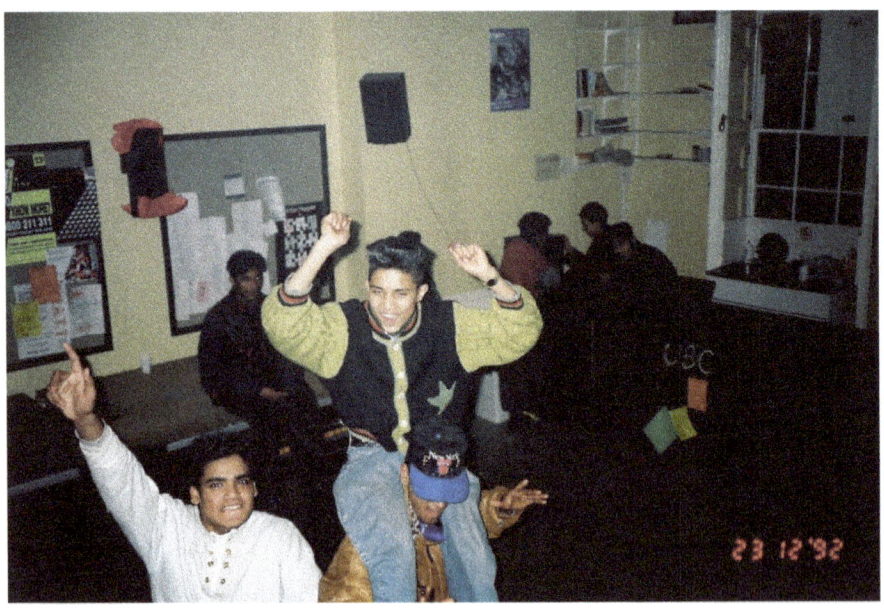

East End Photos, Through Mayar's Eyes : Voluntary Sector 1992-1993

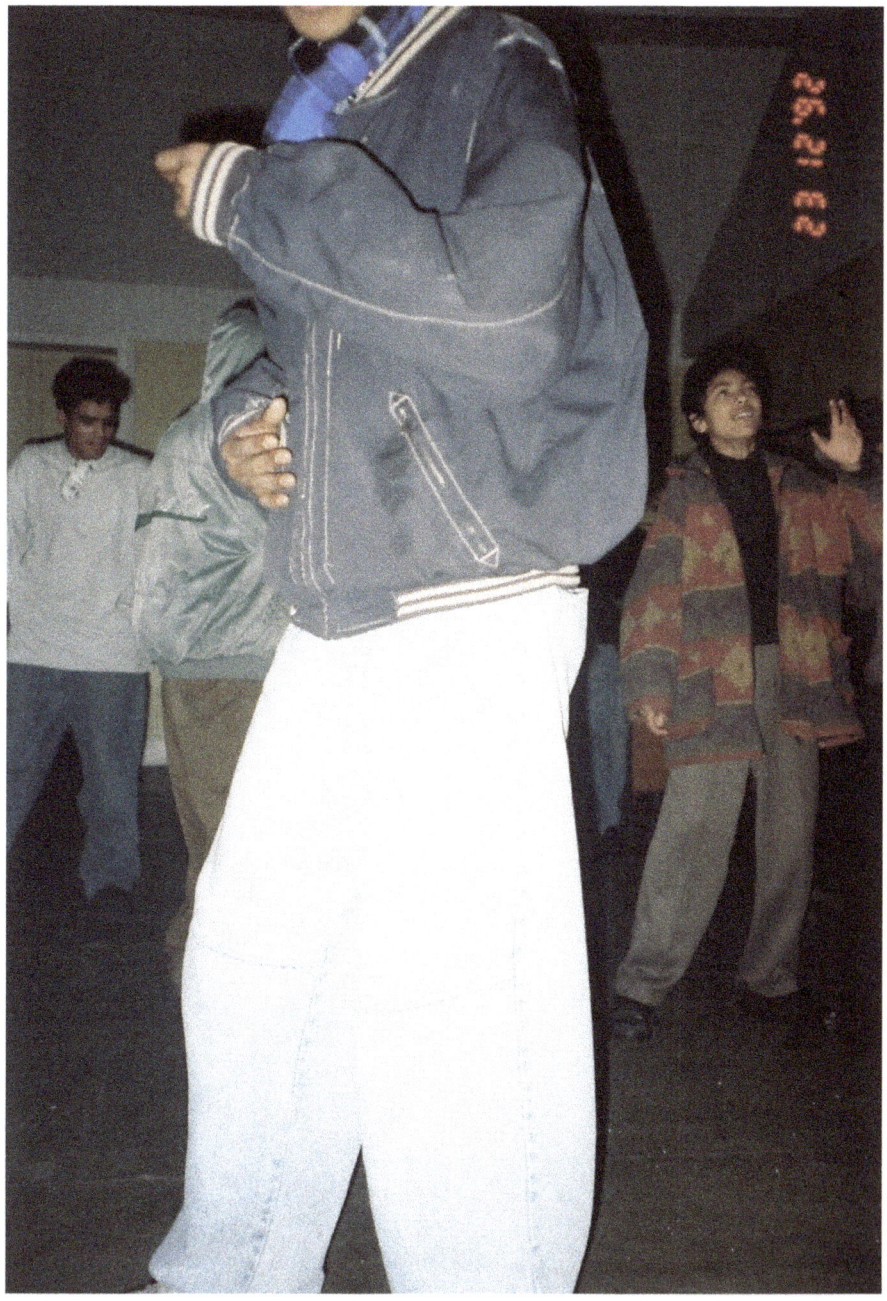

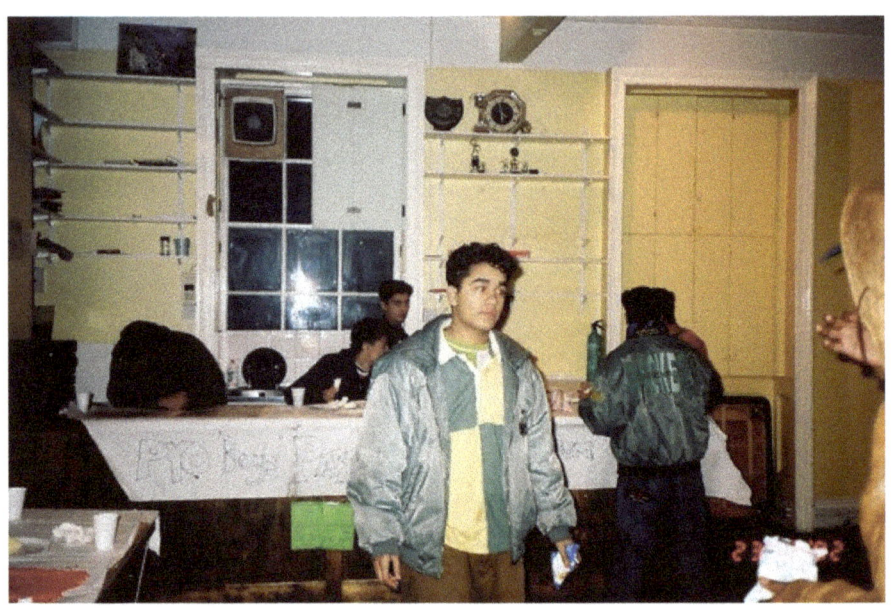

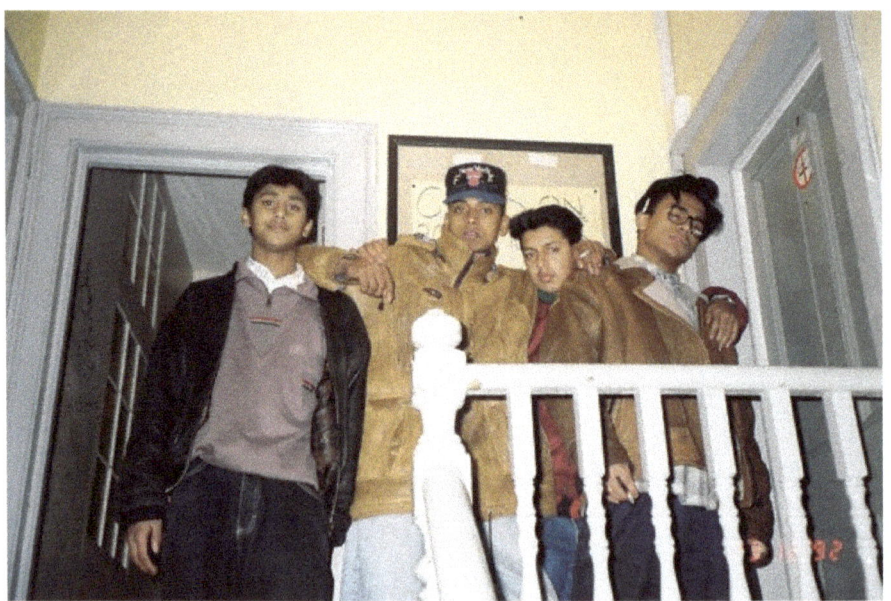

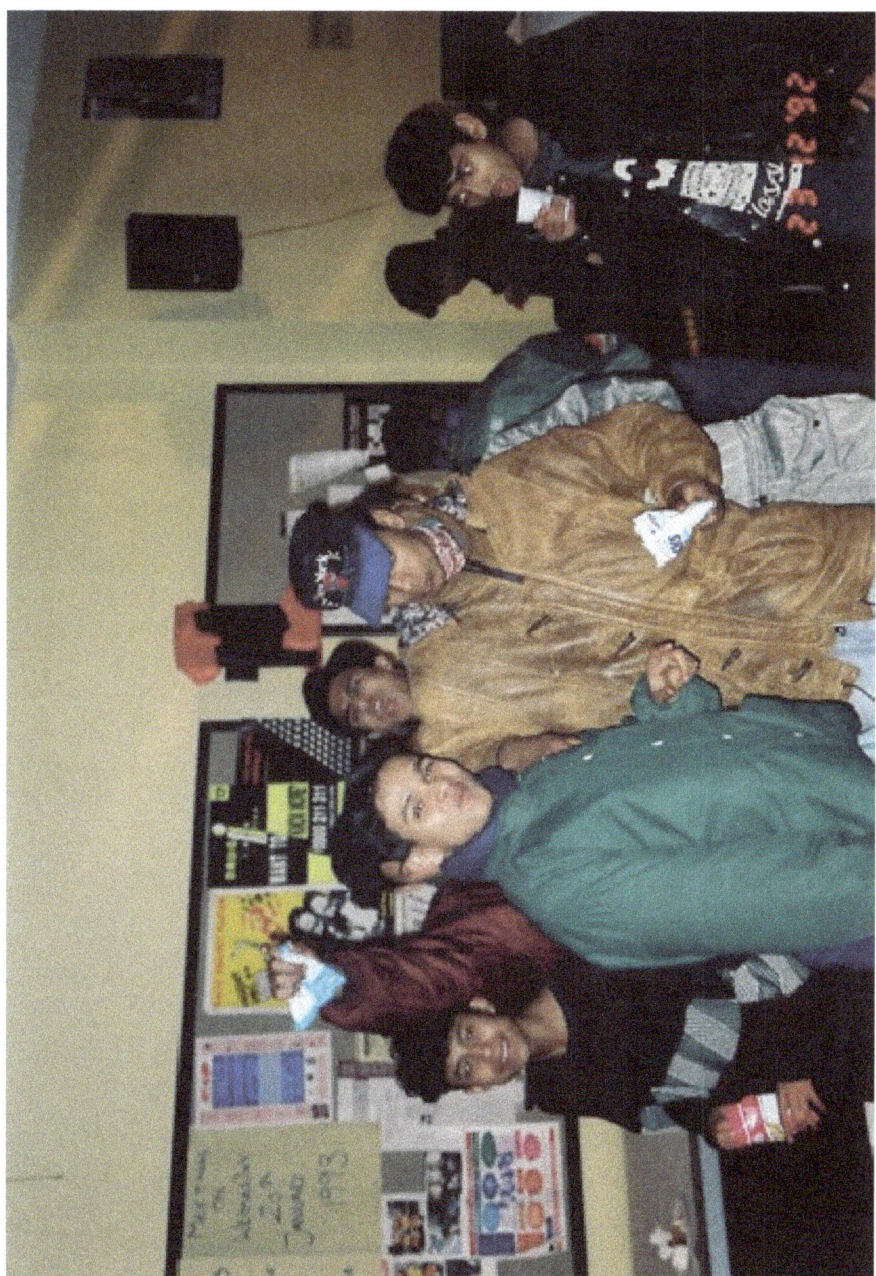

Chand in the background, this would have been a good time to have nurtured him to making a career path move.

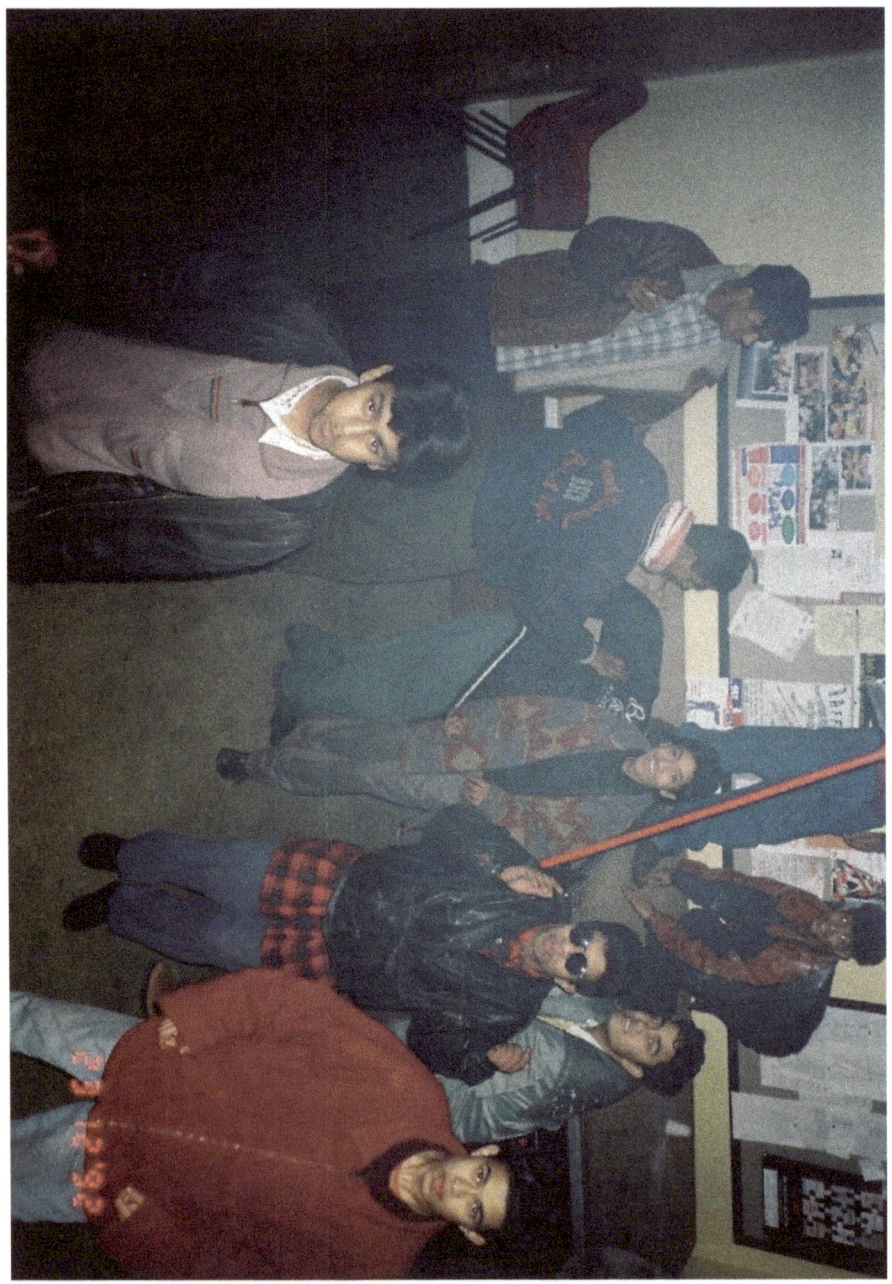

Muktar Ahmed, enjoying himself with his friends

East End Photos, Through Mayar's Eyes : Voluntary Sector 1992-1993

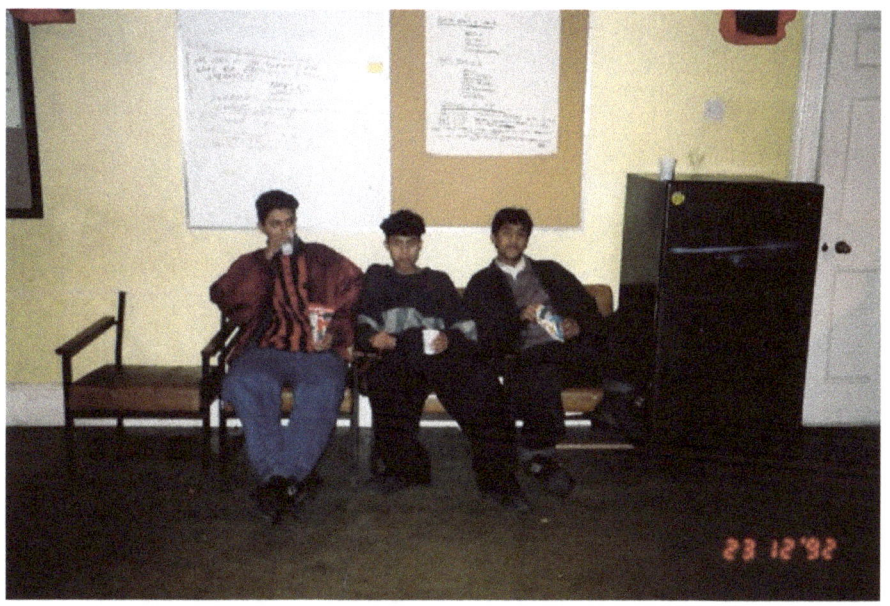

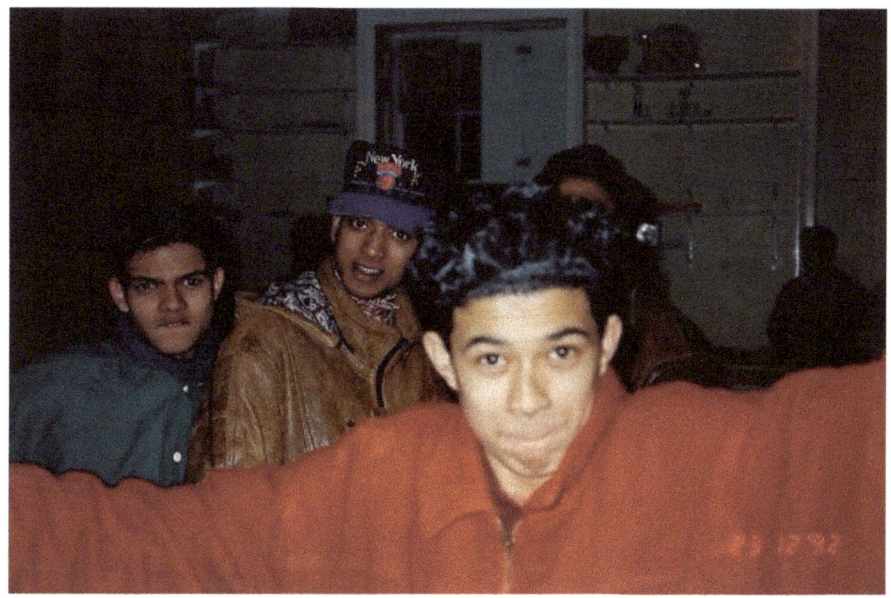

67

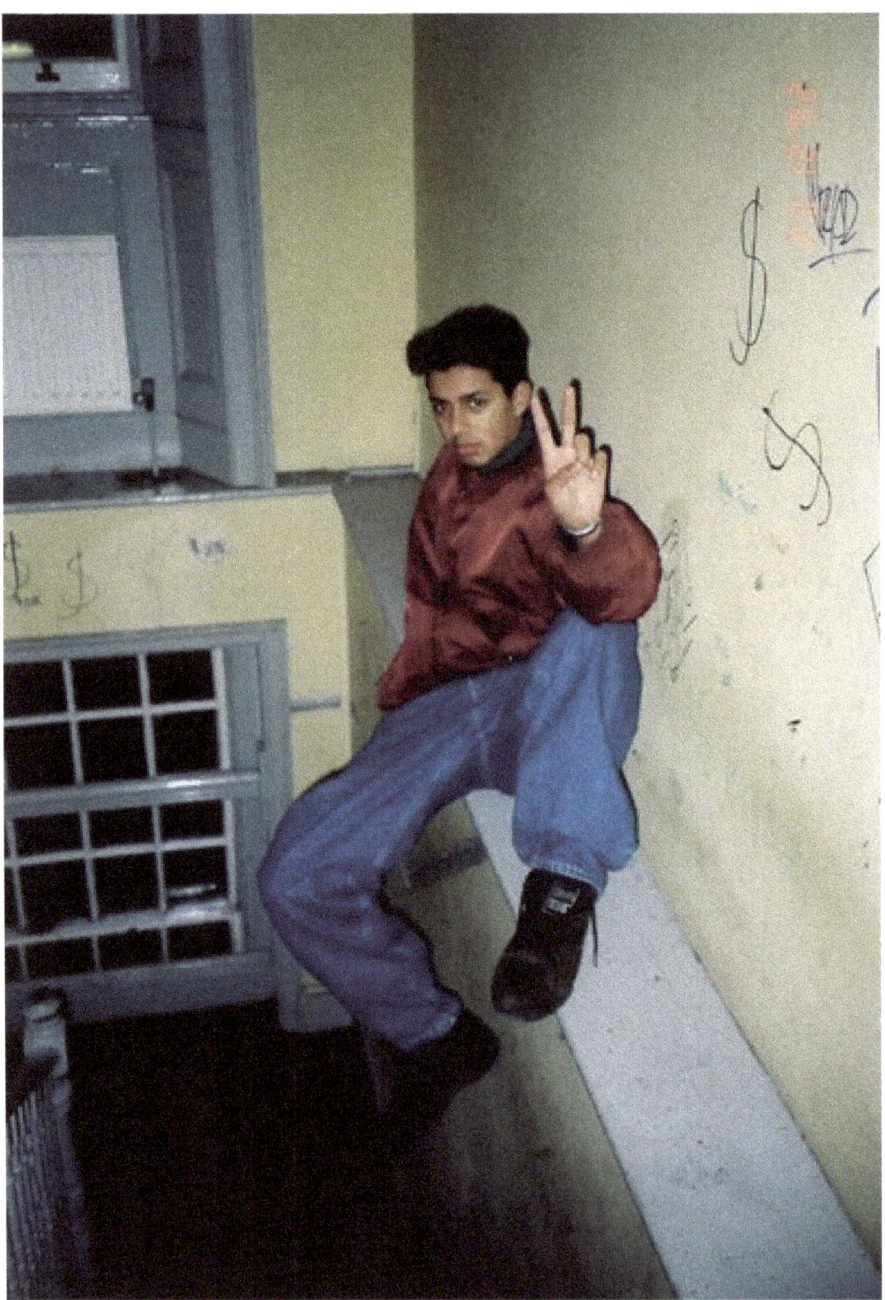

Poser

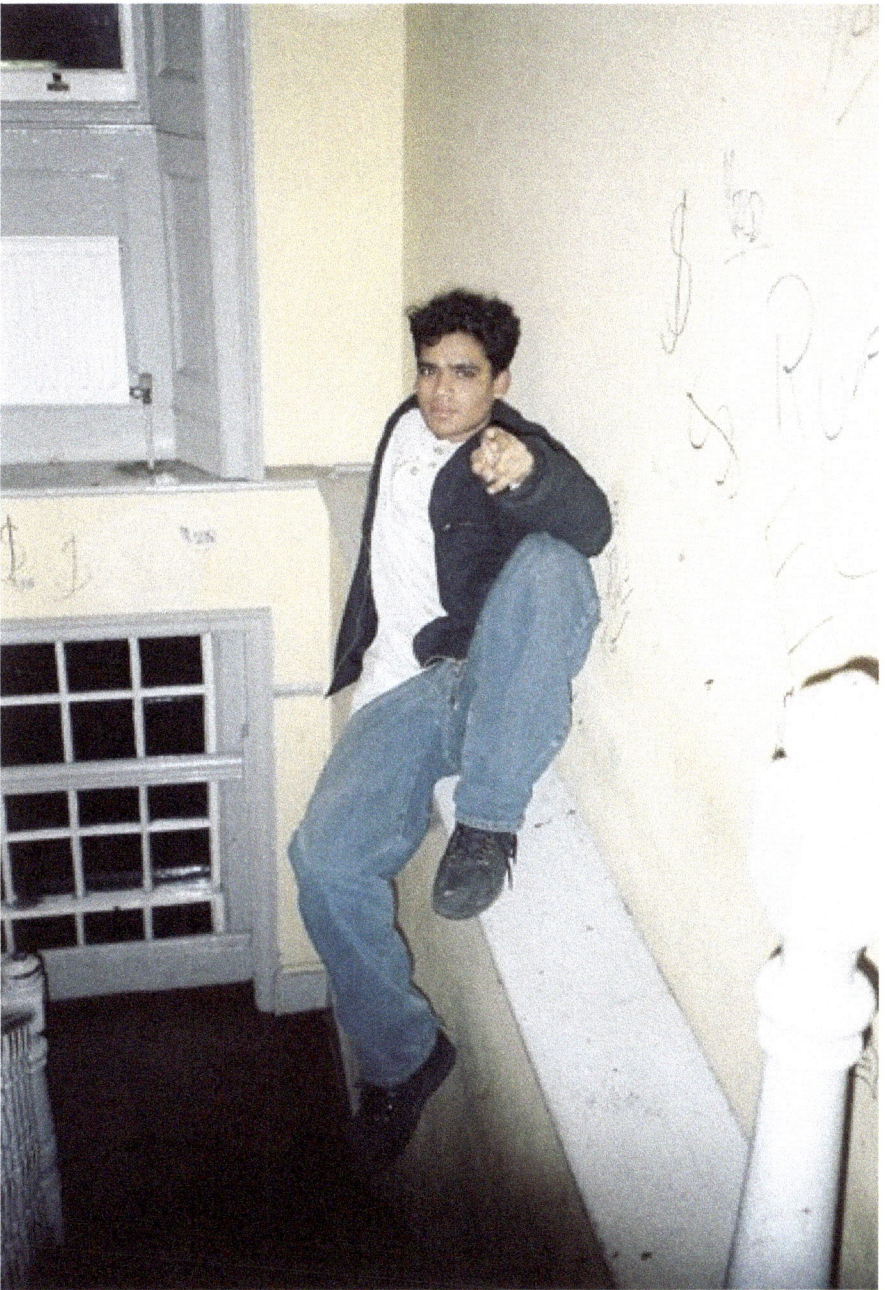

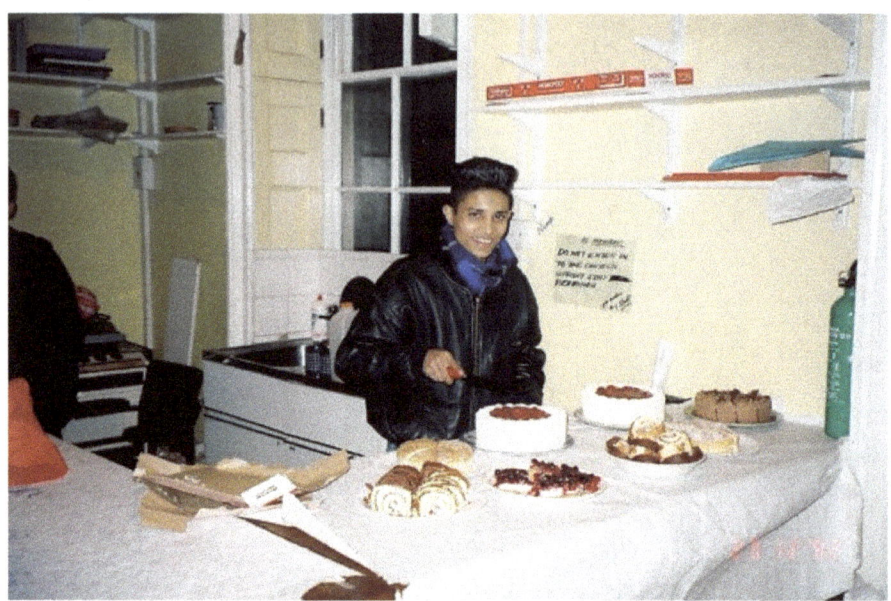

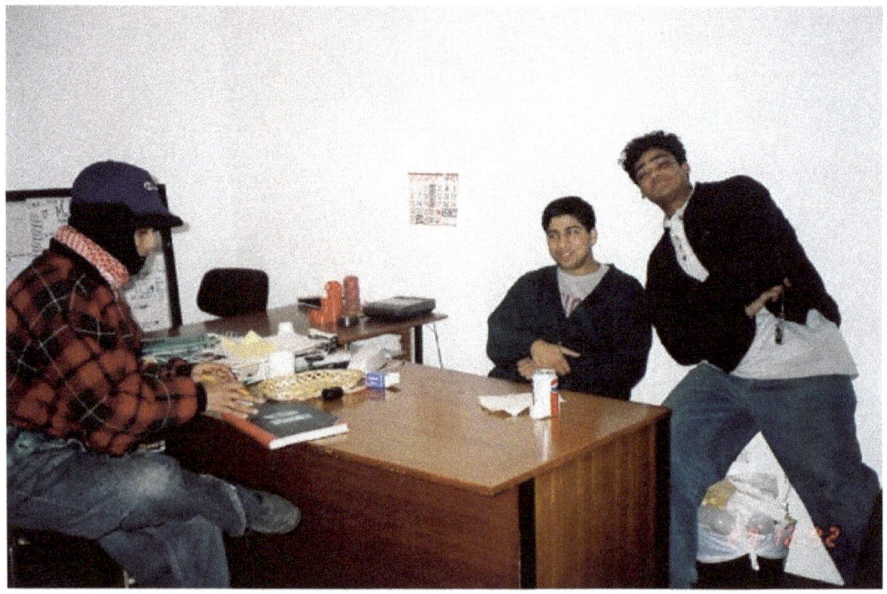

Boys taking a picture of the staff team, Salik Hussain, Senior youth worker and me in the head gear.

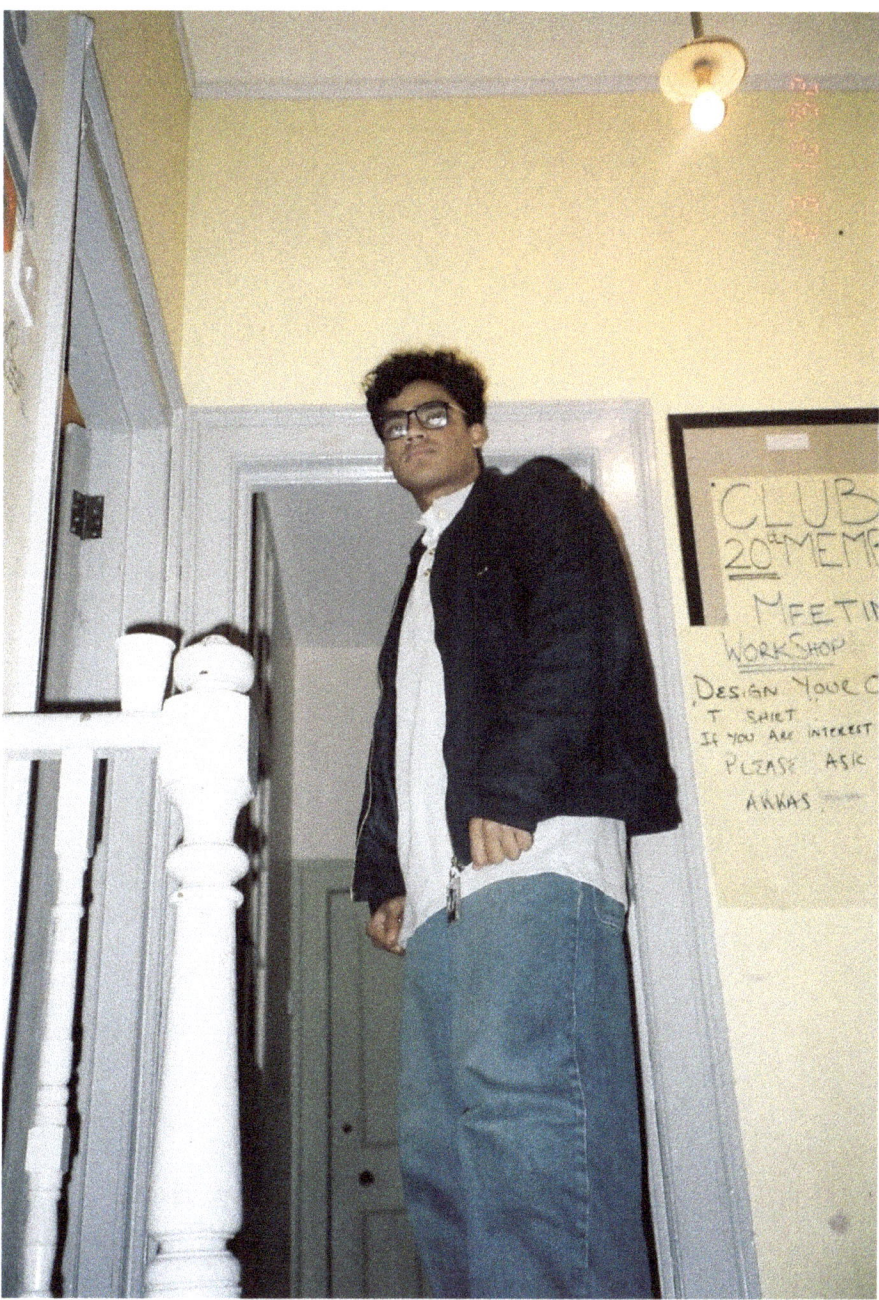

Turon da boffin LOLZ

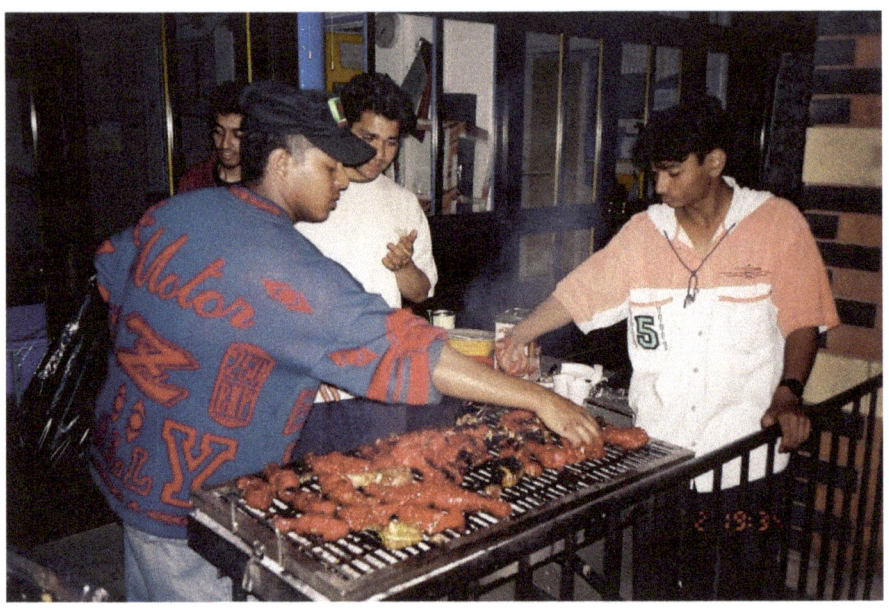

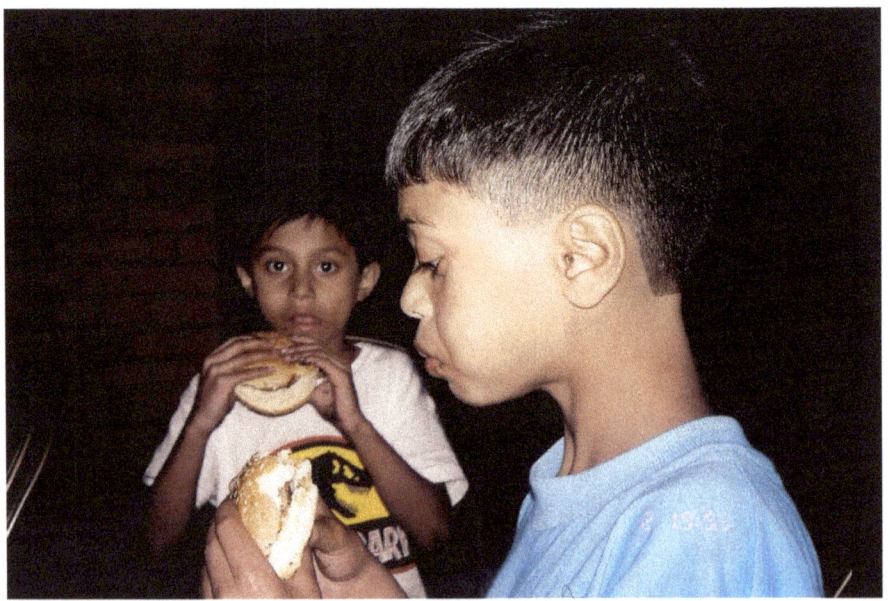

Hmm, what you saying?

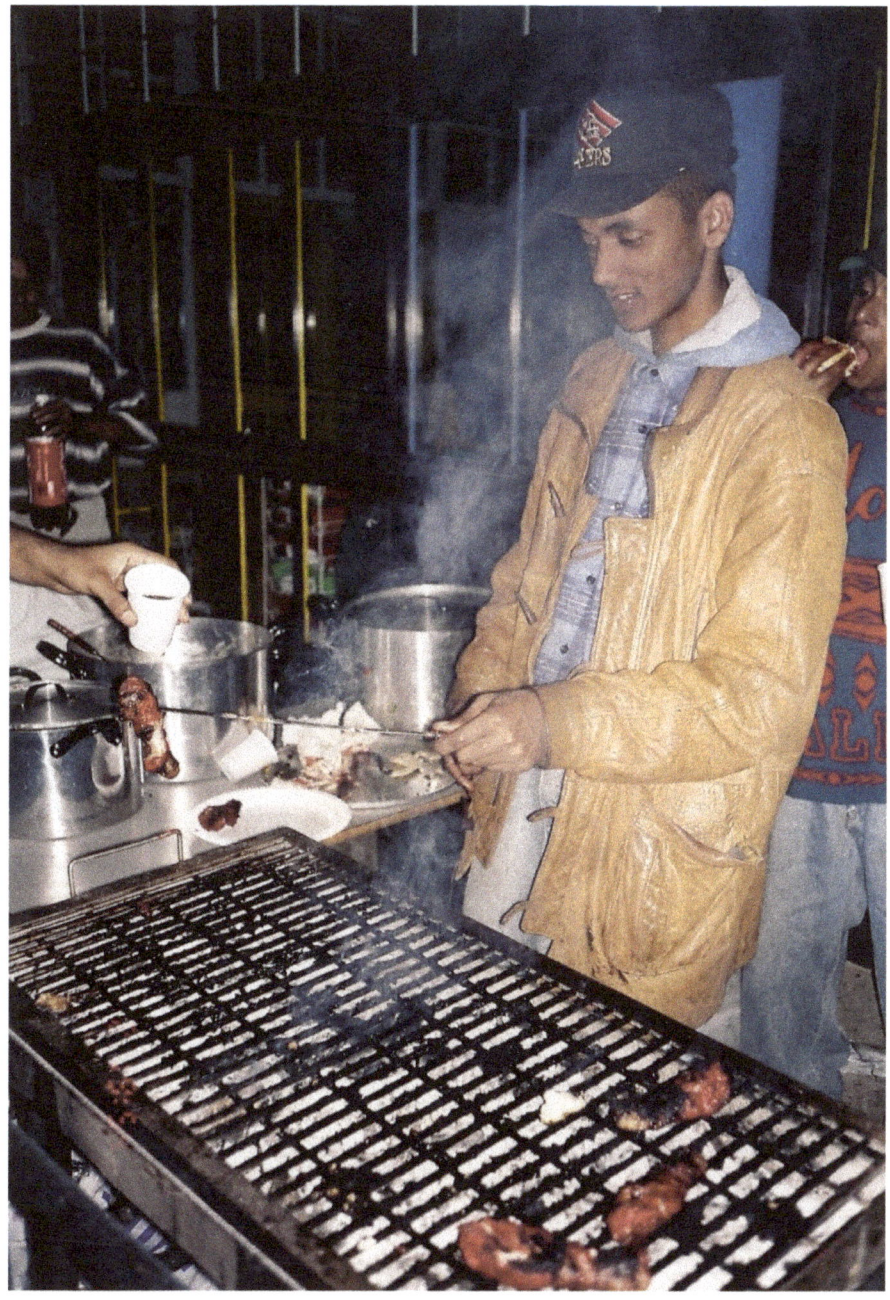

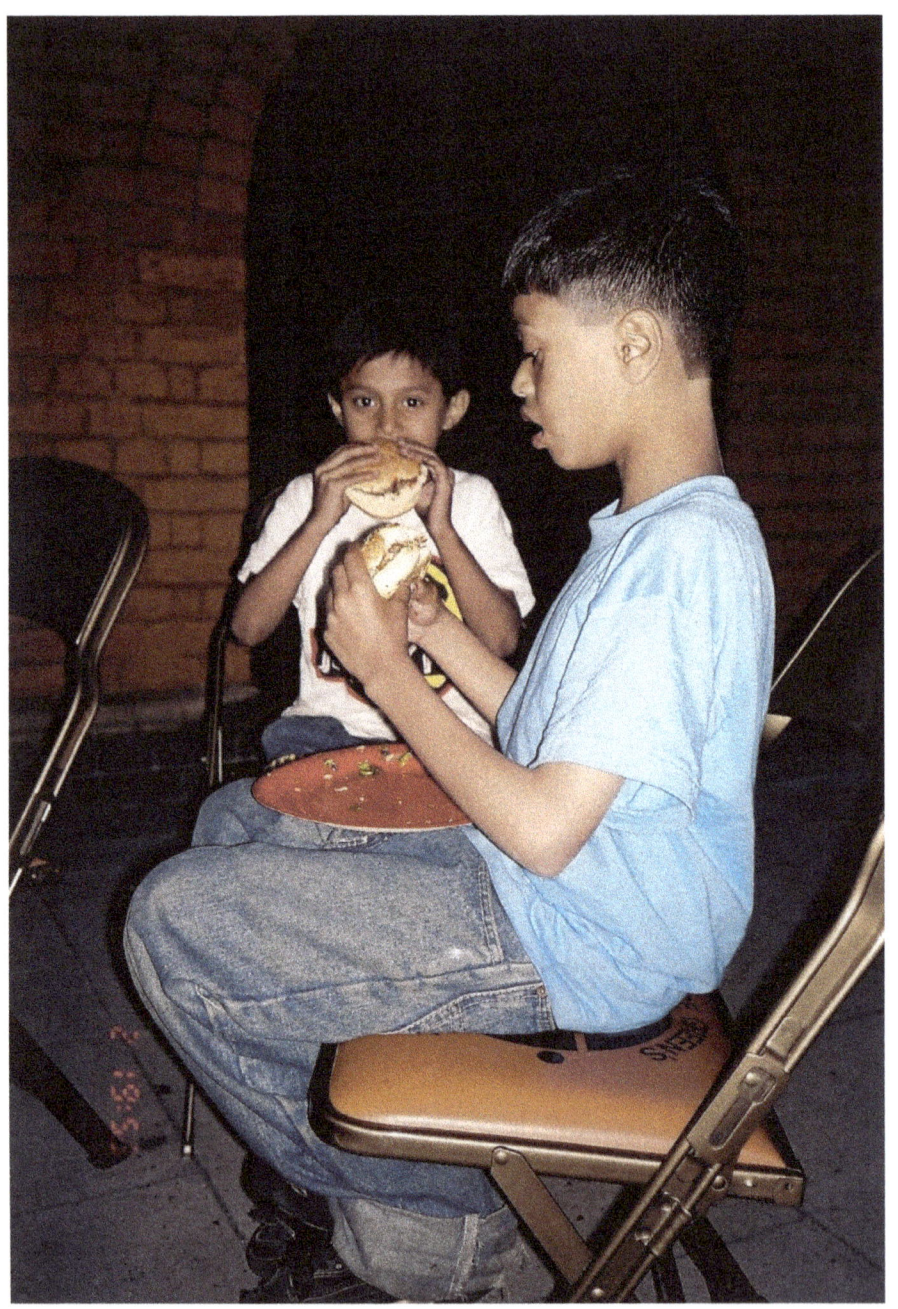

Let me eat you lol!!!

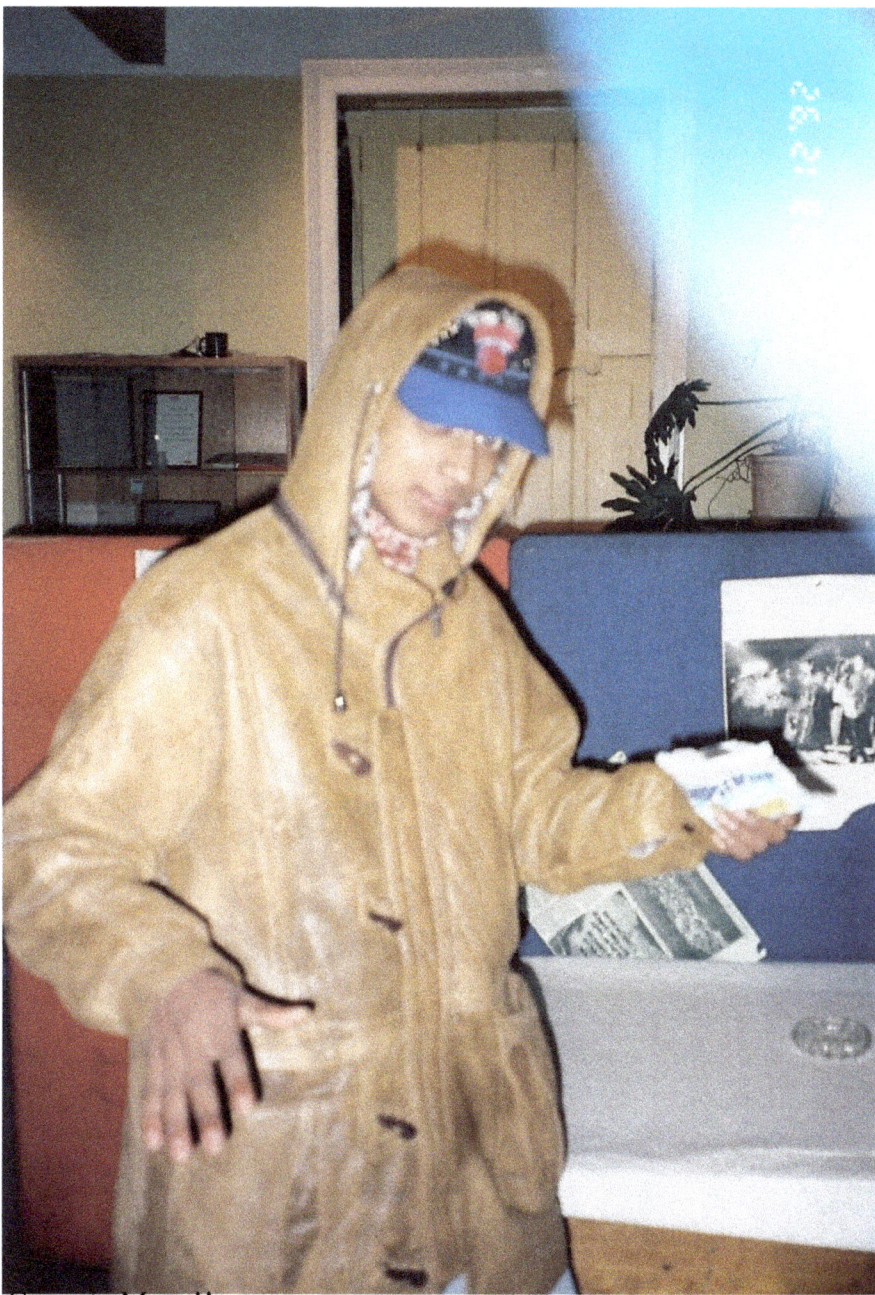

Gangsta Manz!!

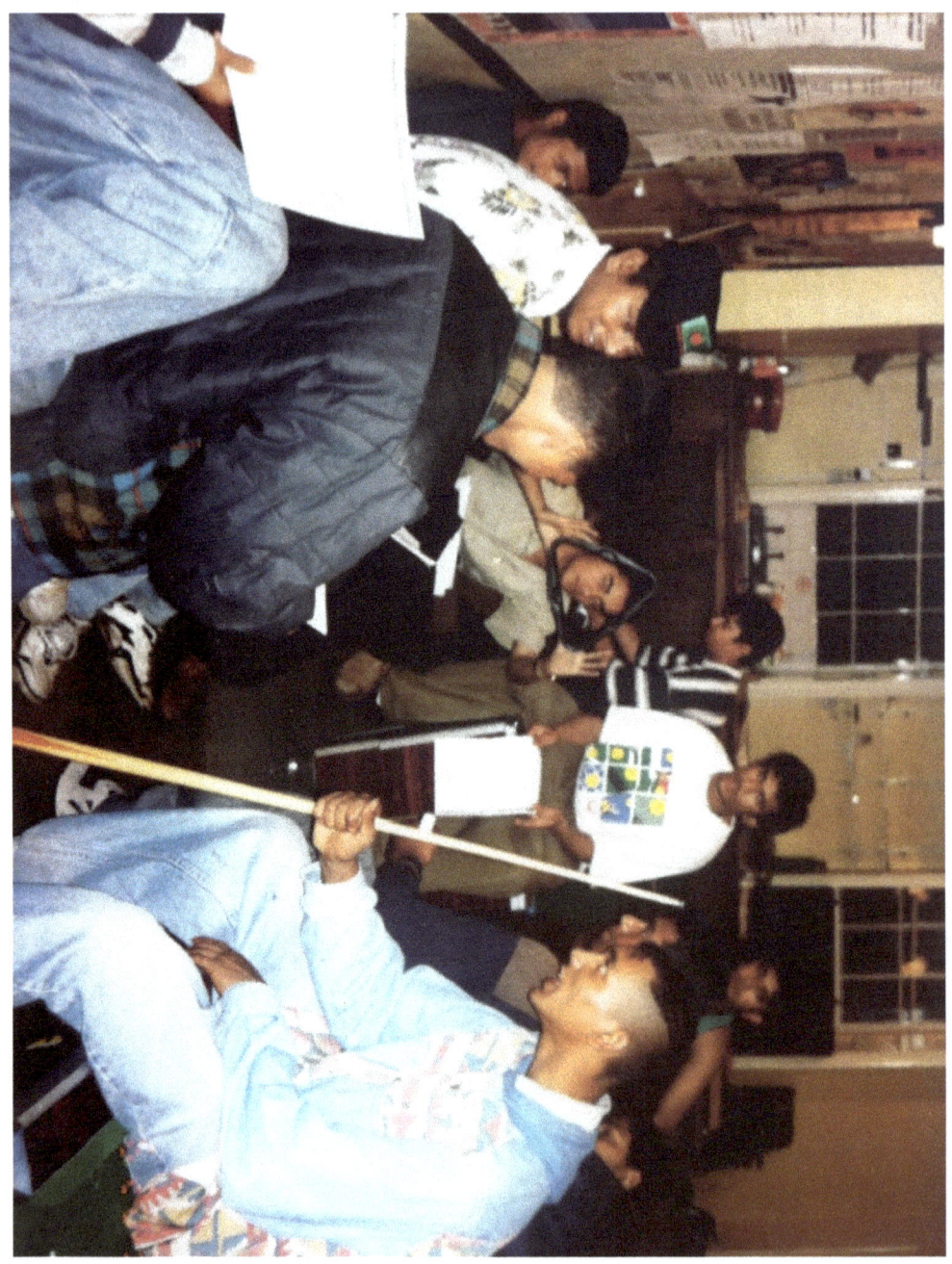

East End Photos, Through Mayar's Eyes : Voluntary Sector 1992-1993

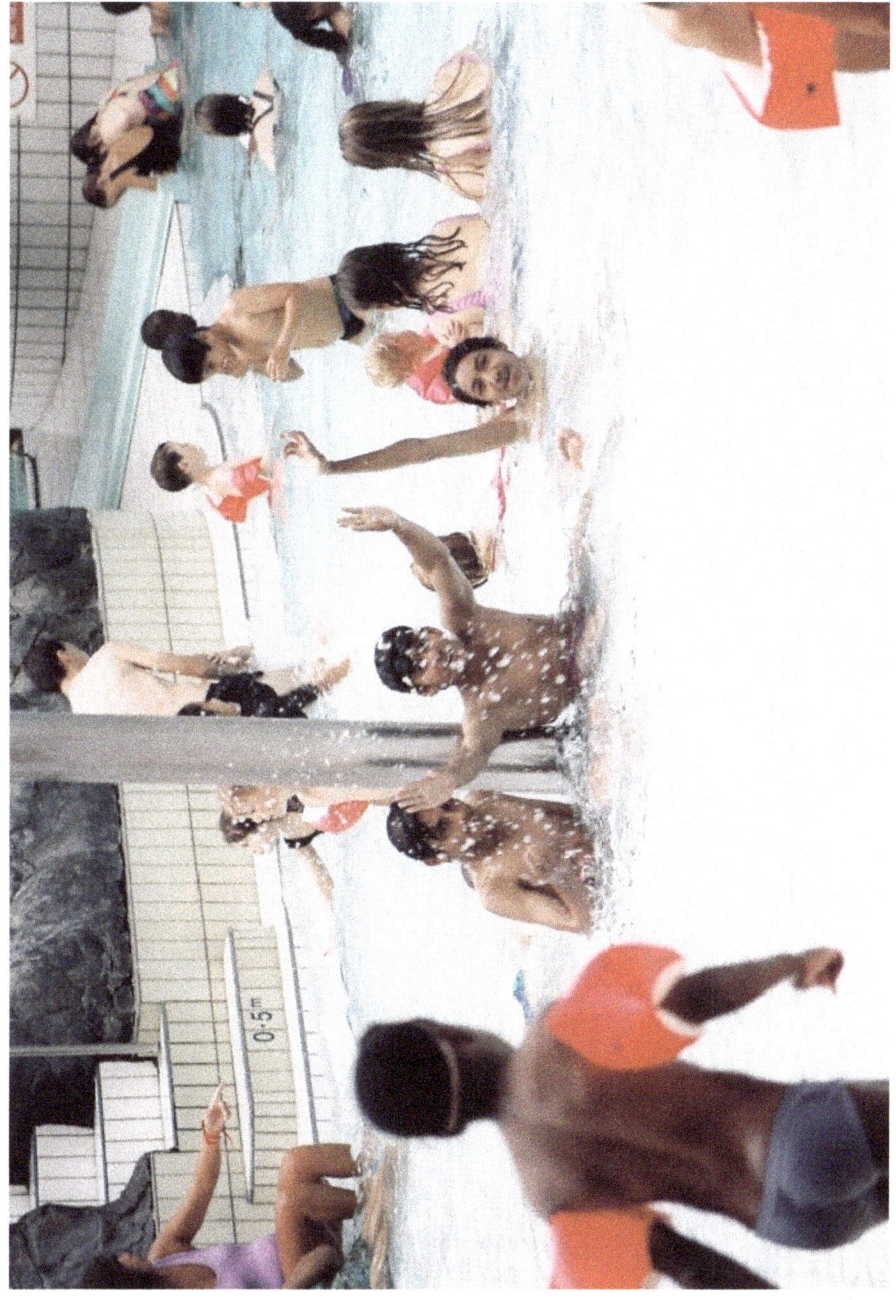

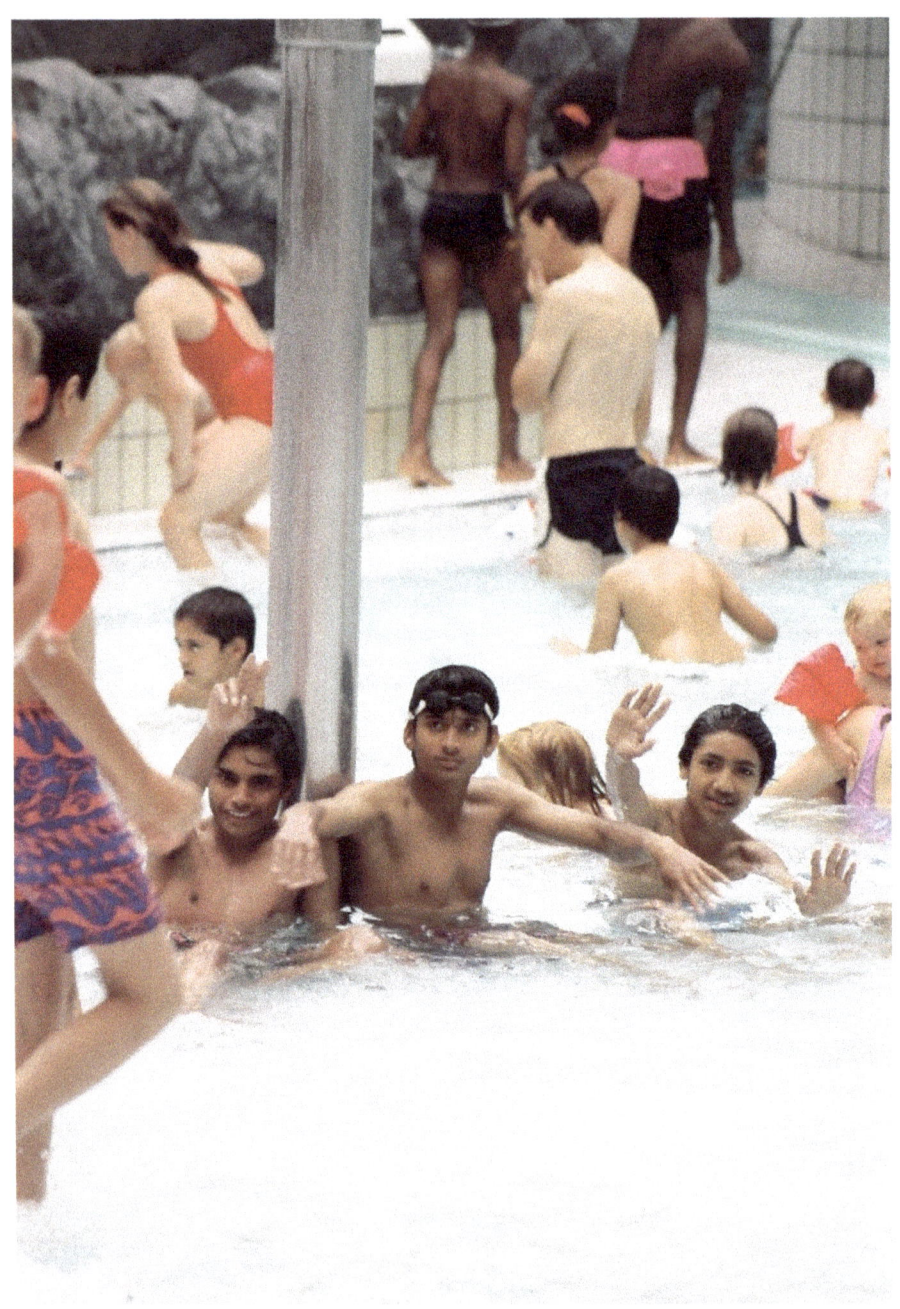

JPYO Swimming in Waterworld!

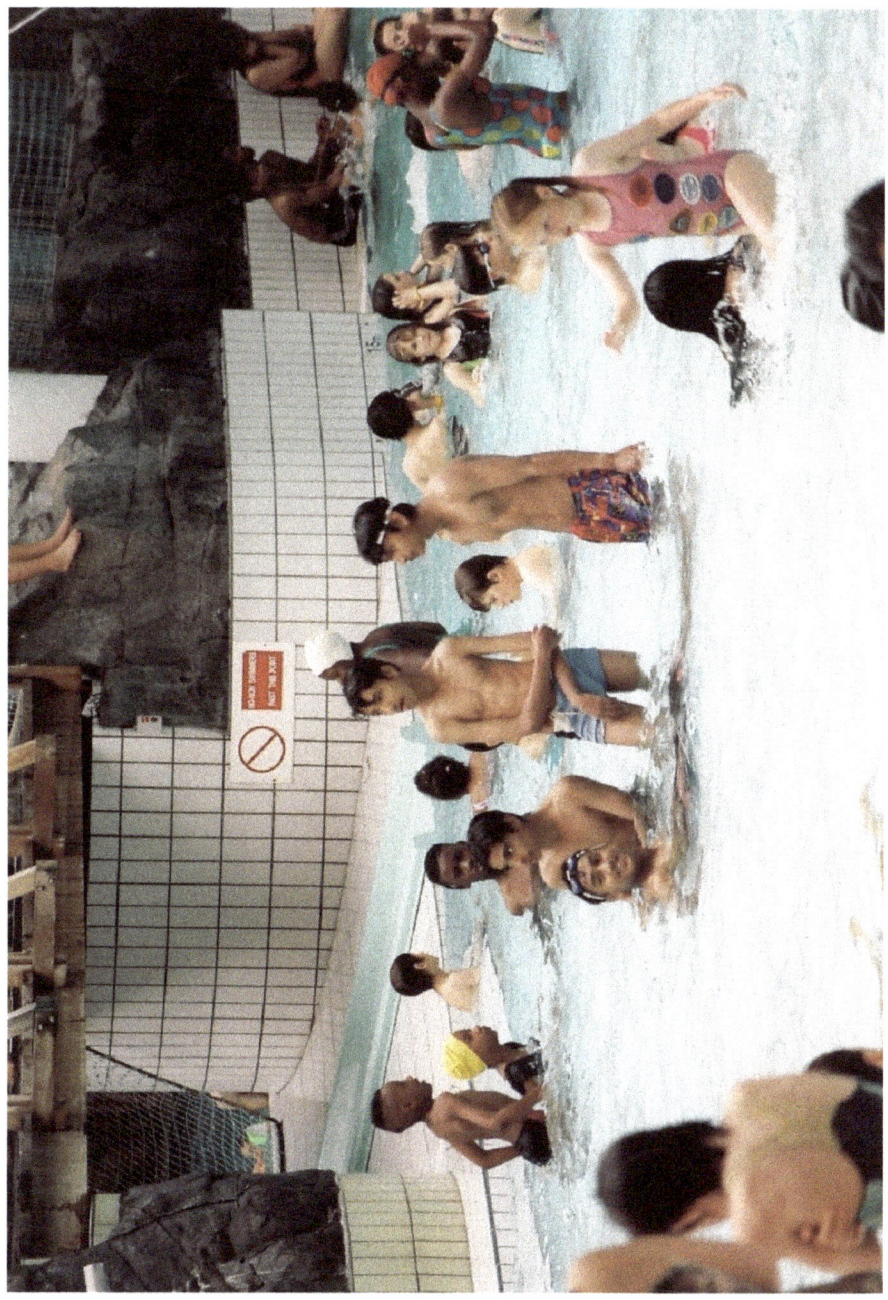

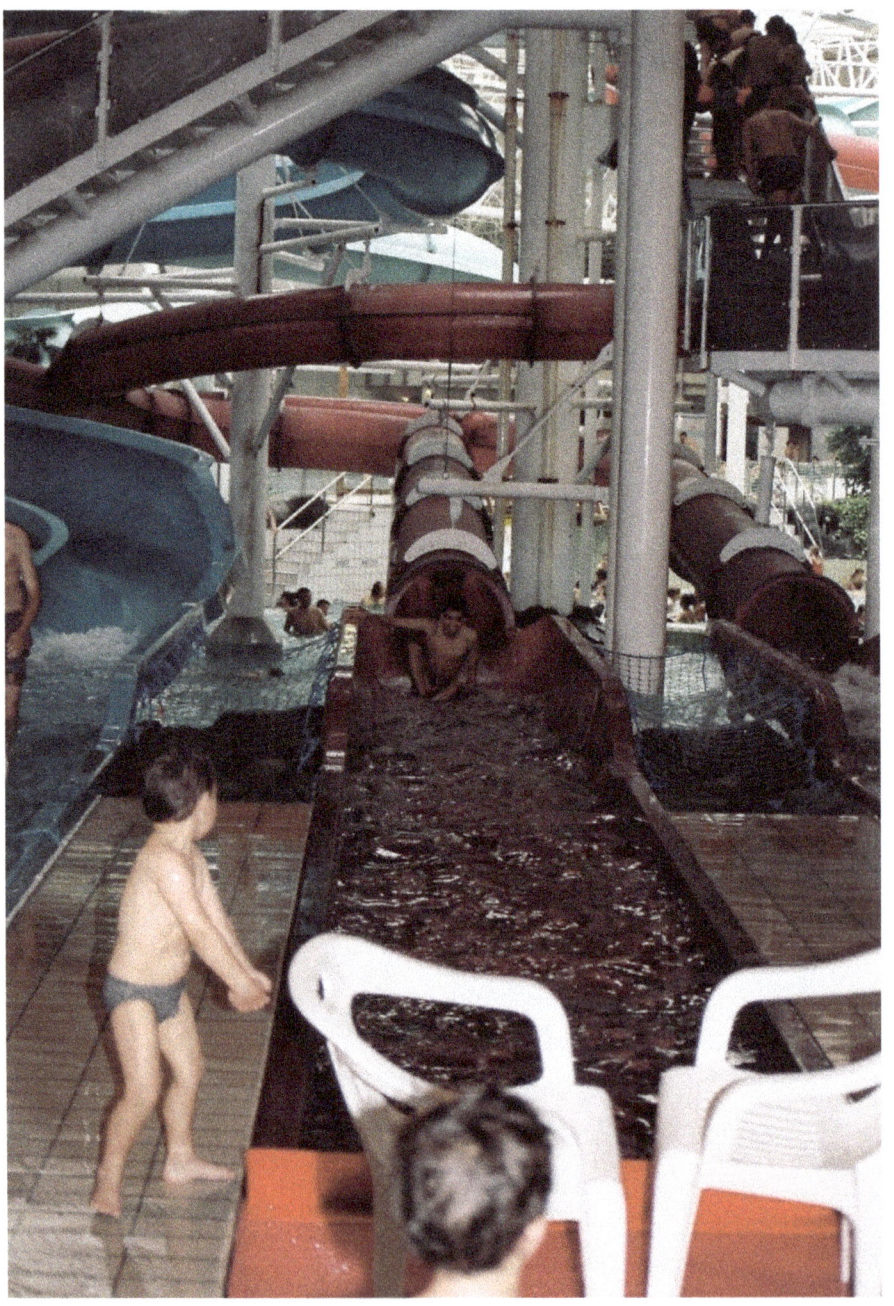

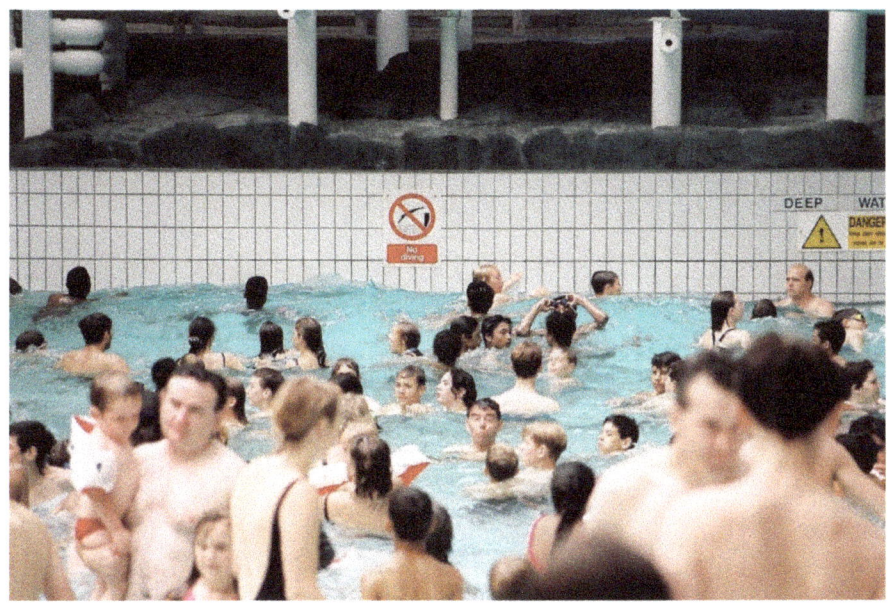

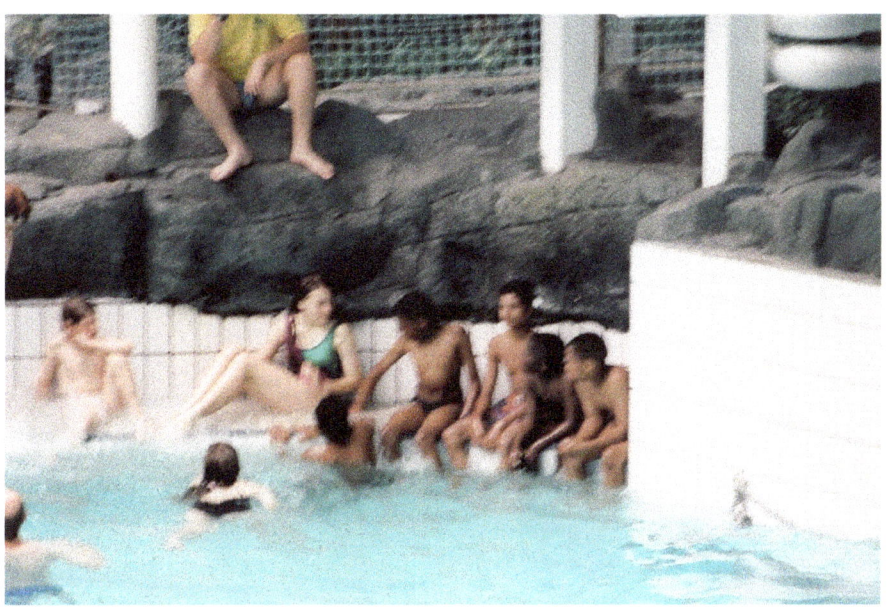

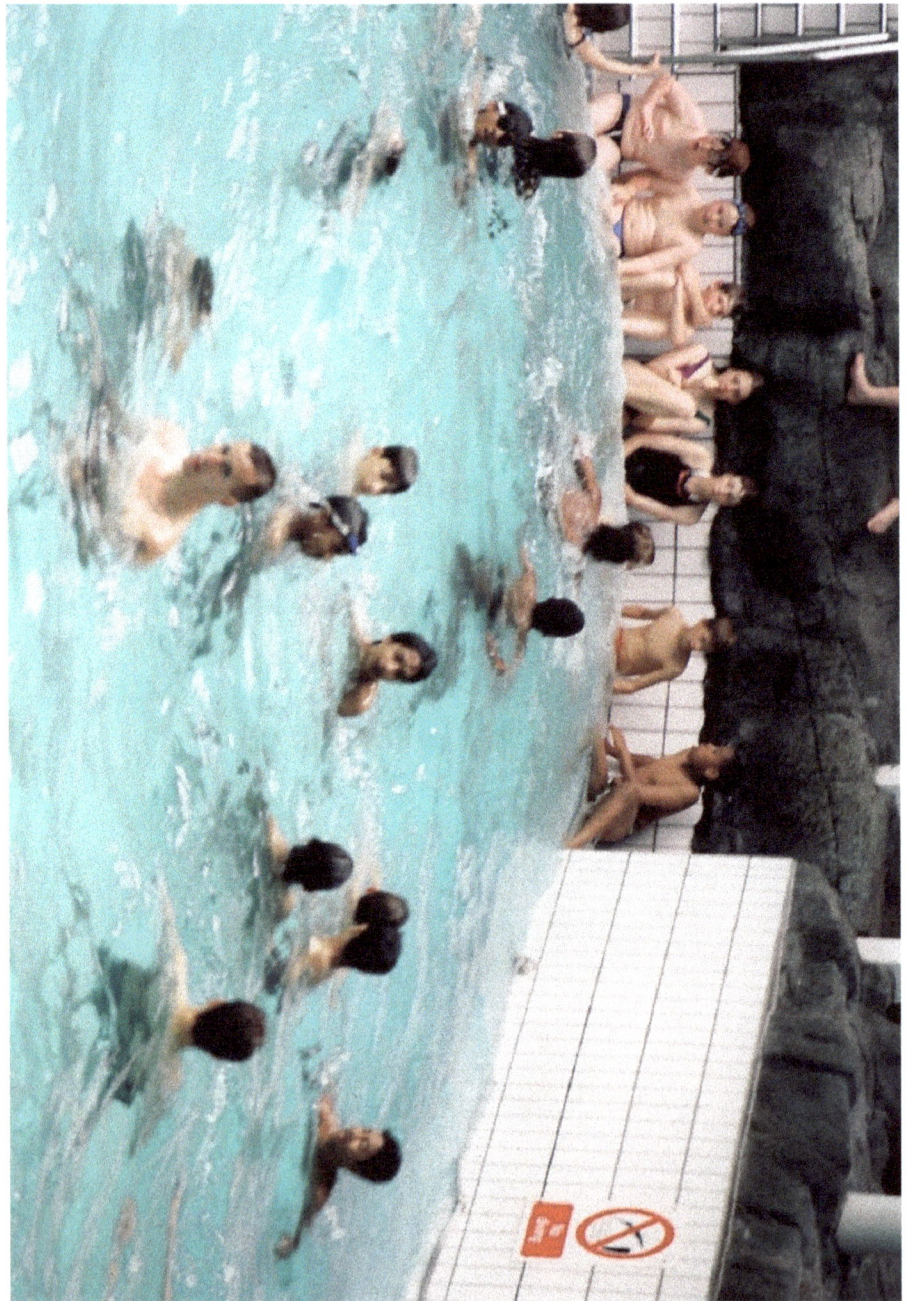

East End Photos, Through Mayar's Eyes : Voluntary Sector 1992-1993

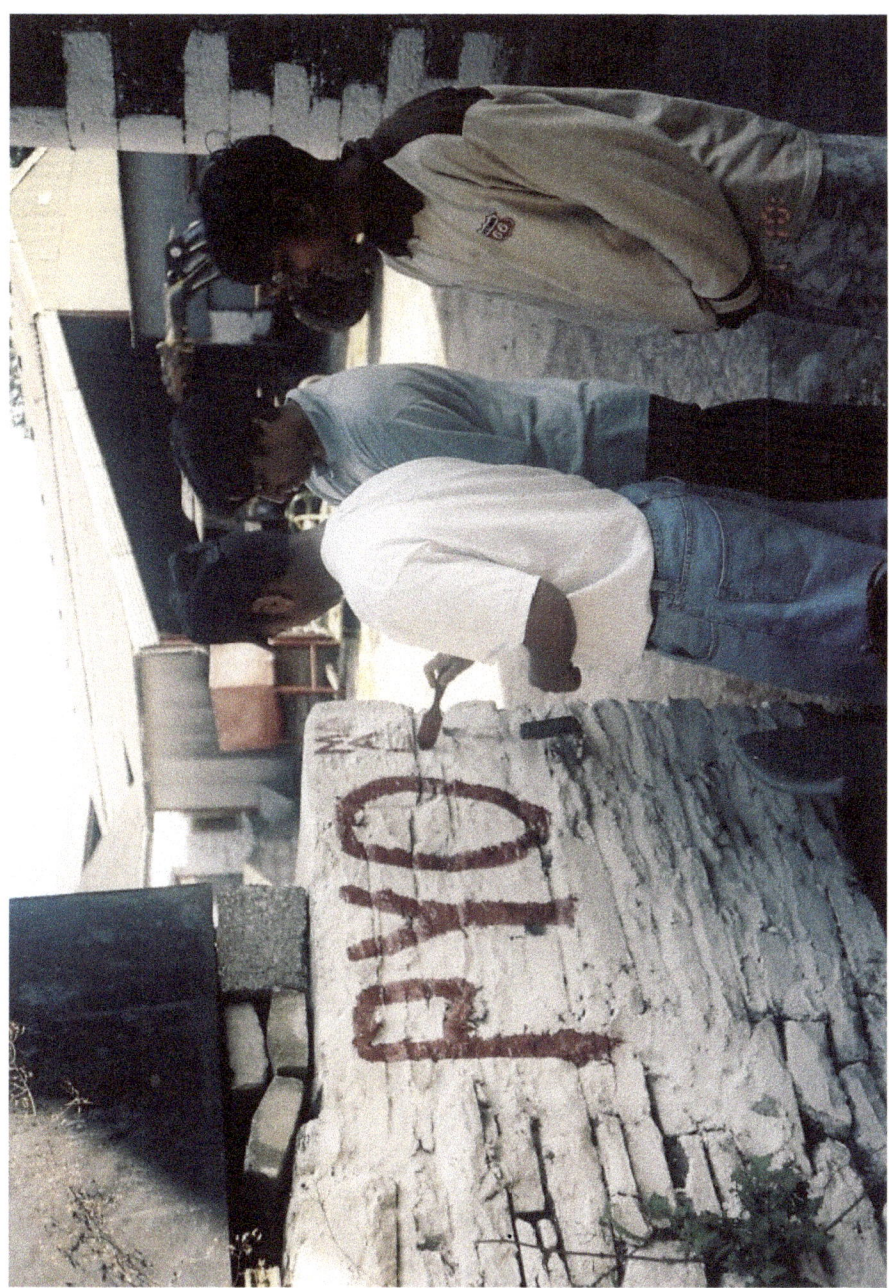

Residential In Wales

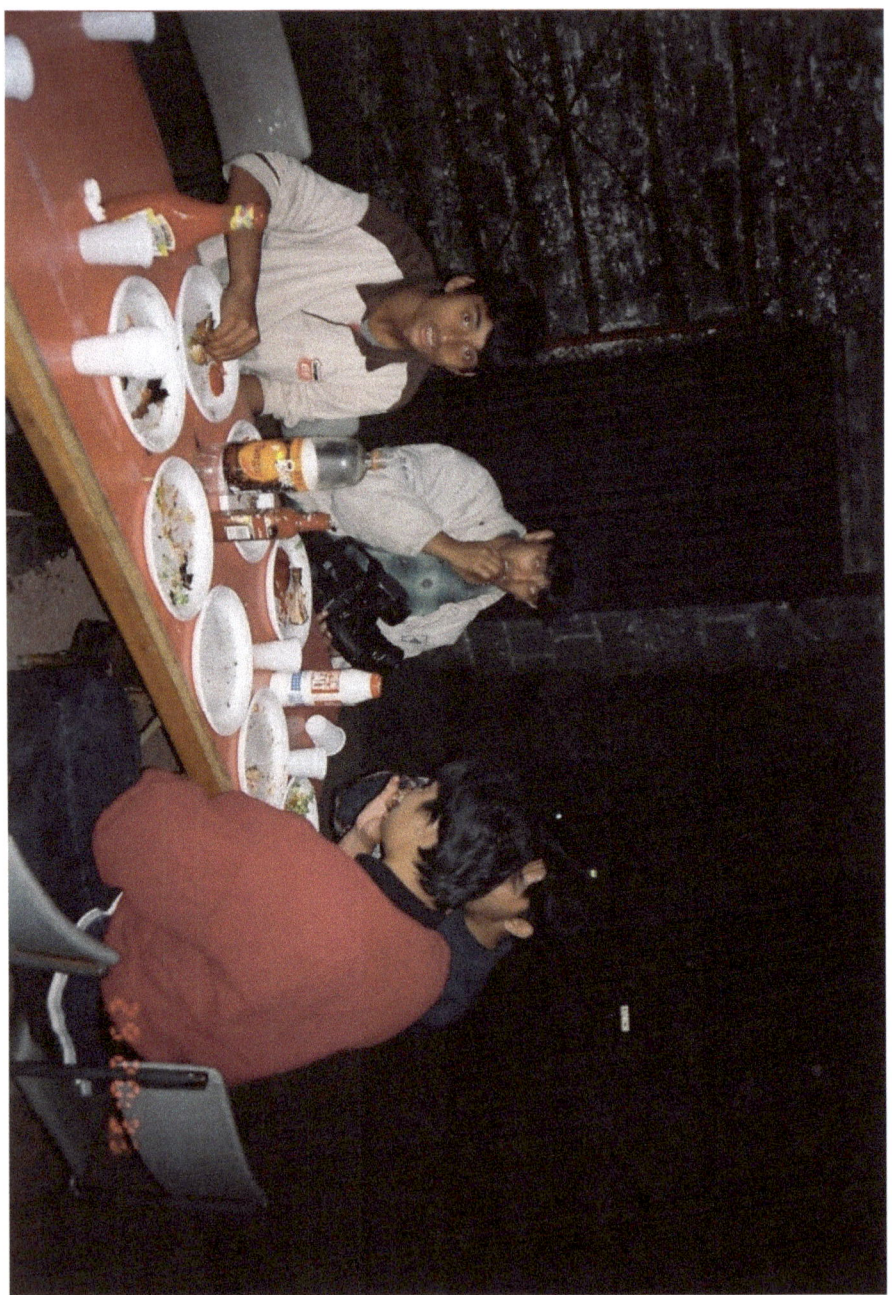

Sharing a meal with the boys

East End Photos, Through Mayar's Eyes : Voluntary Sector 1992-1993

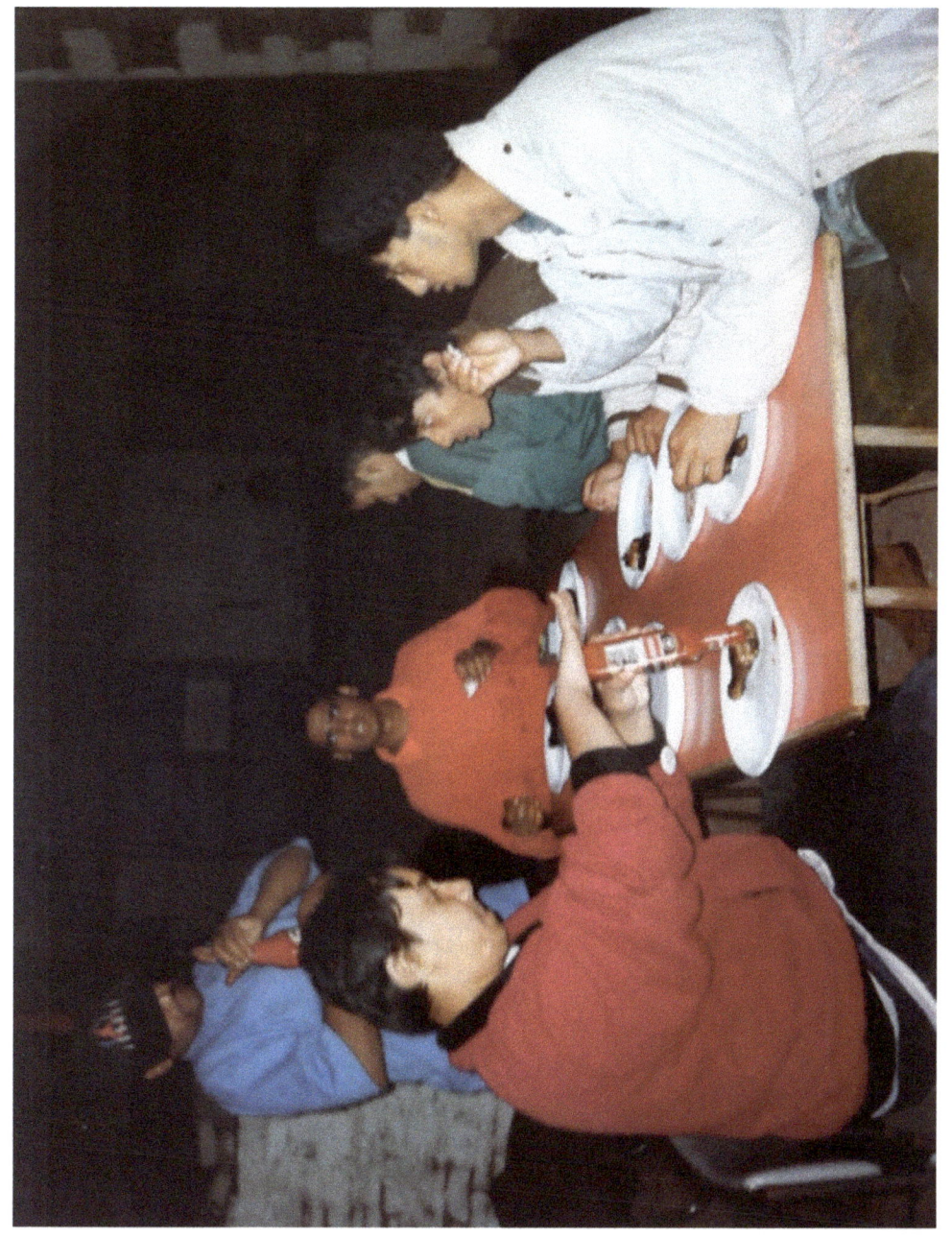

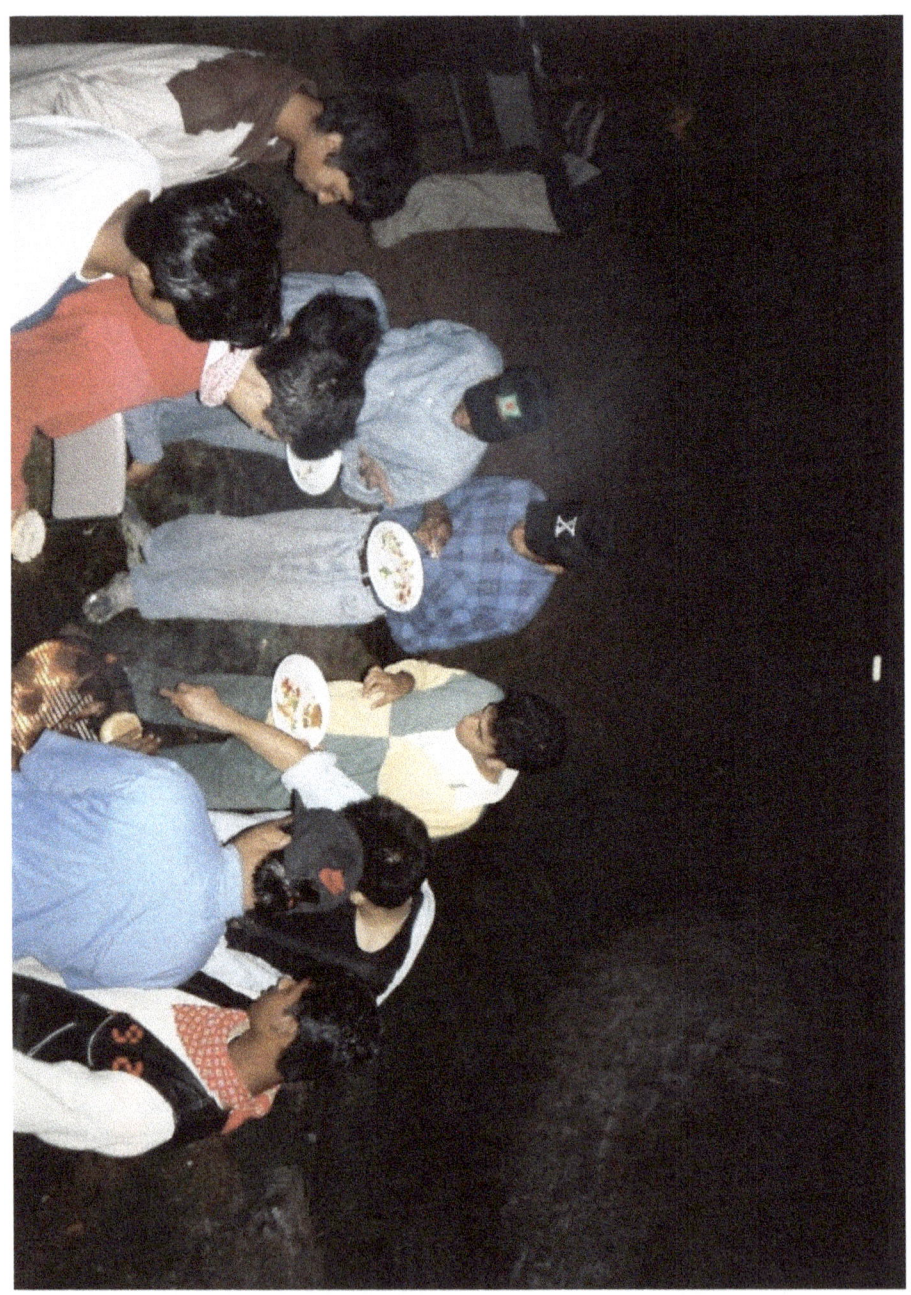

Standing around the BBQ and feasting away!

East End Photos, Through Mayar's Eyes : Voluntary Sector 1992-1993

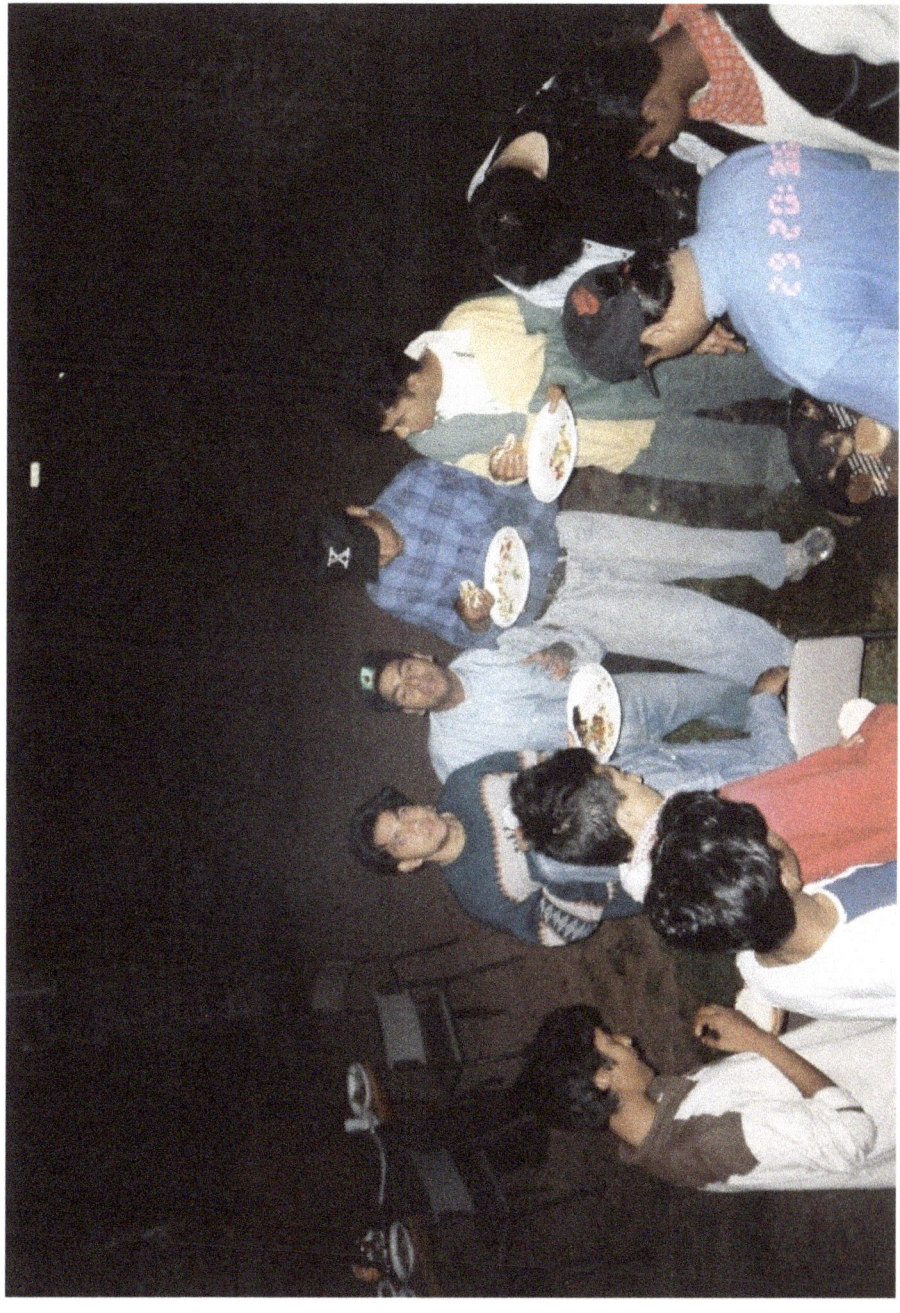

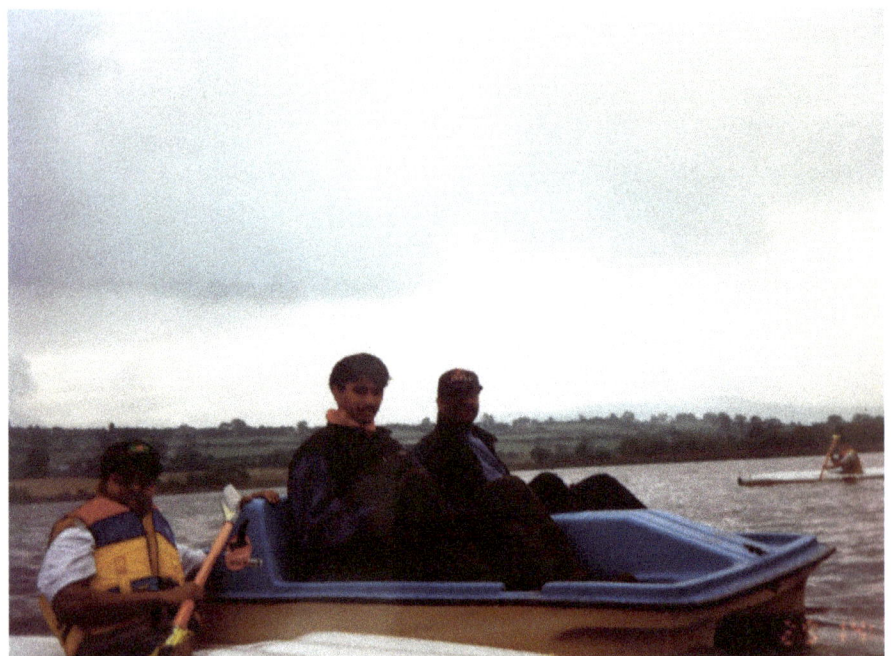

Local activities

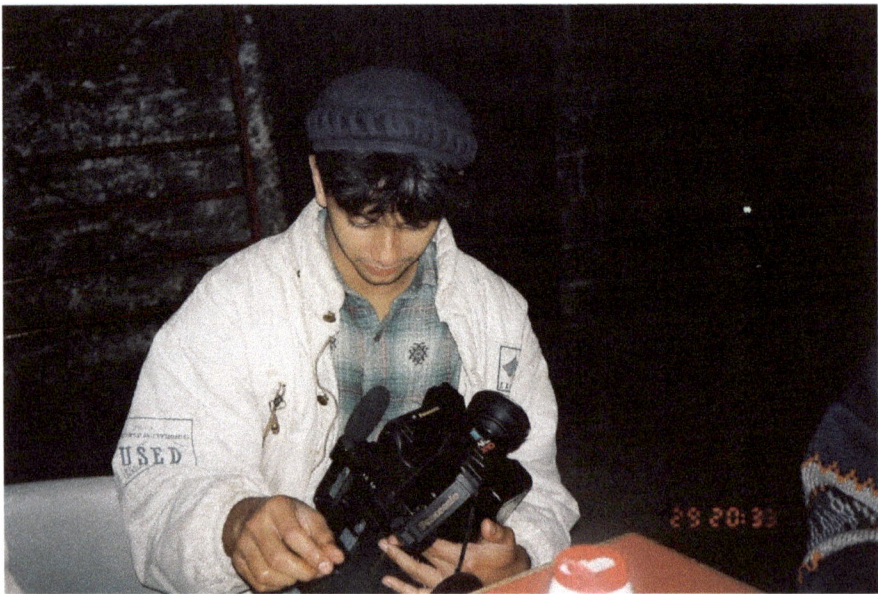

Camera reversed on me.

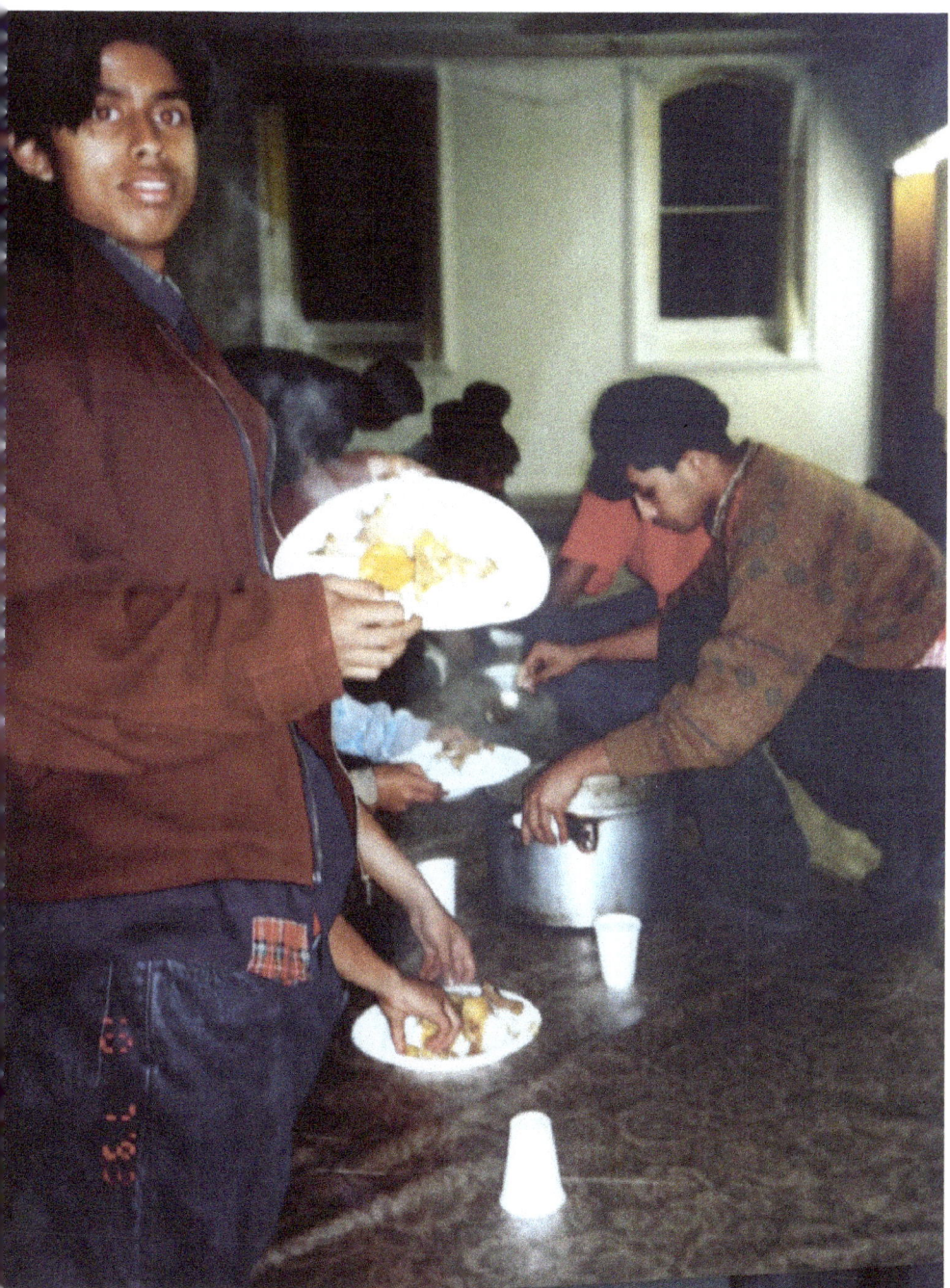

10.7.1993 - Residential to Darul Ummah

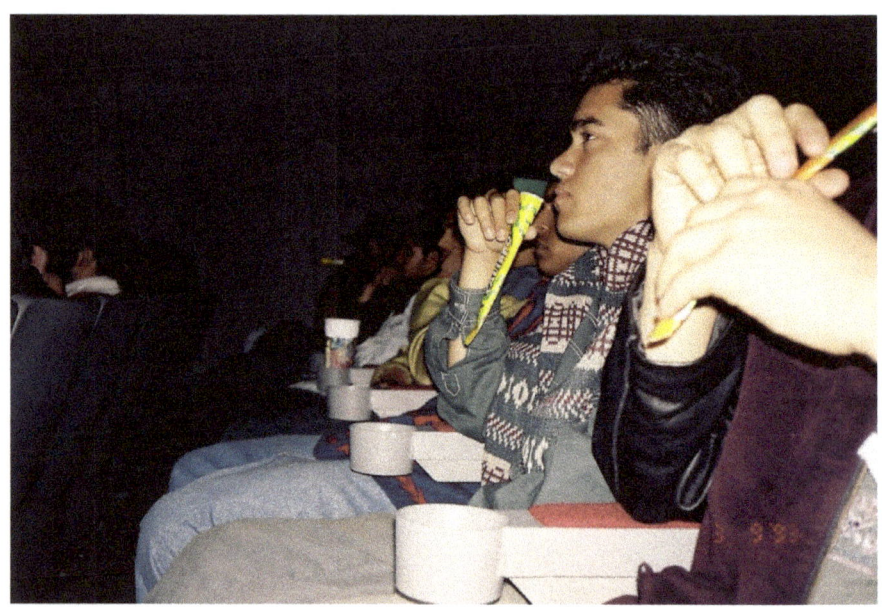

Cinema trip as part of the Summer holiday activity, 3.9.1993

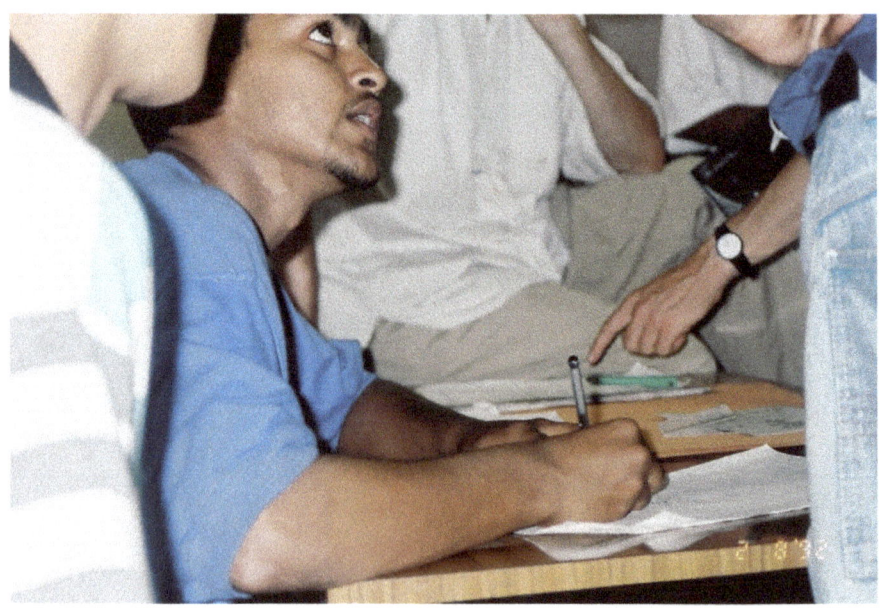

Collingwood Volunteers 2.8.1992

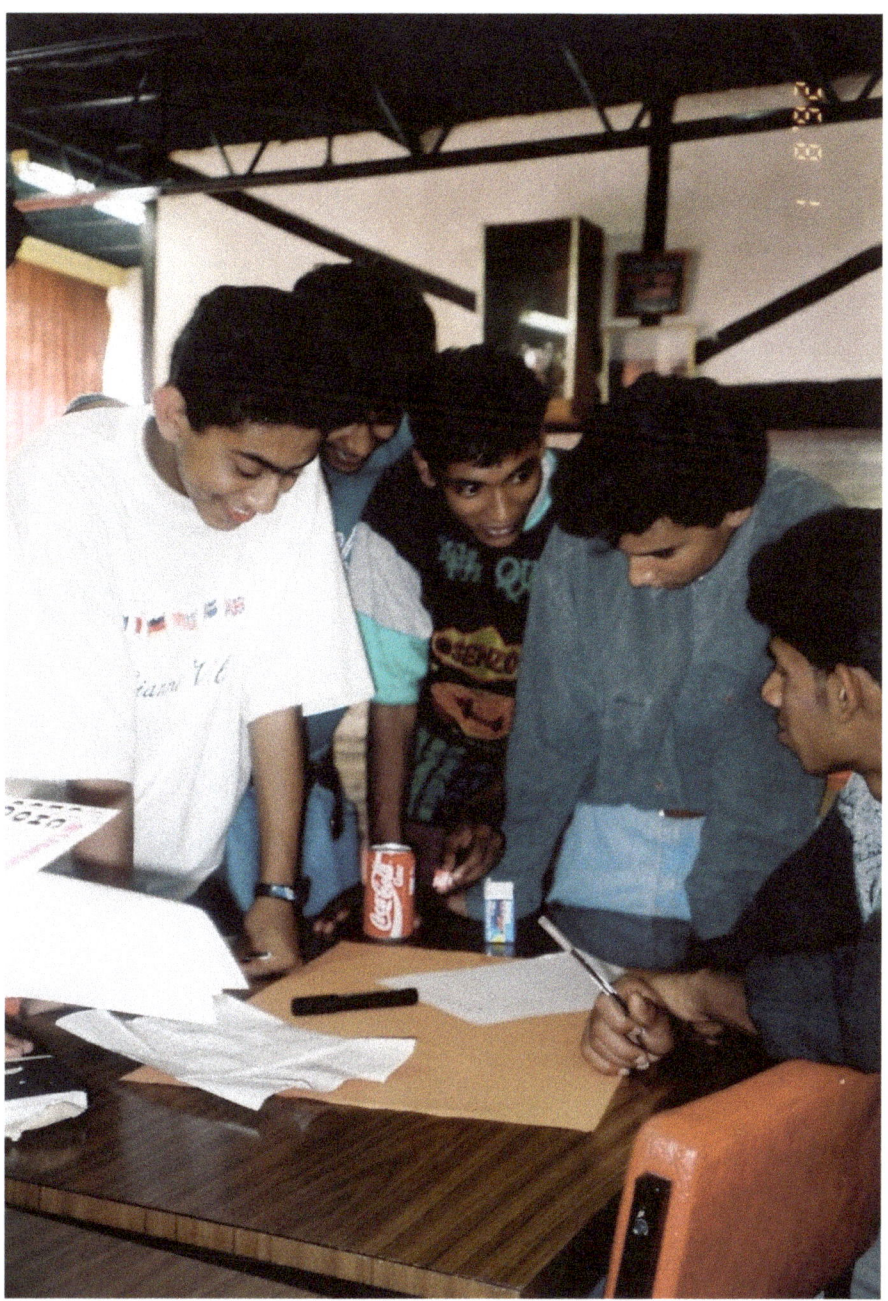

Group work training, 1.8.1992

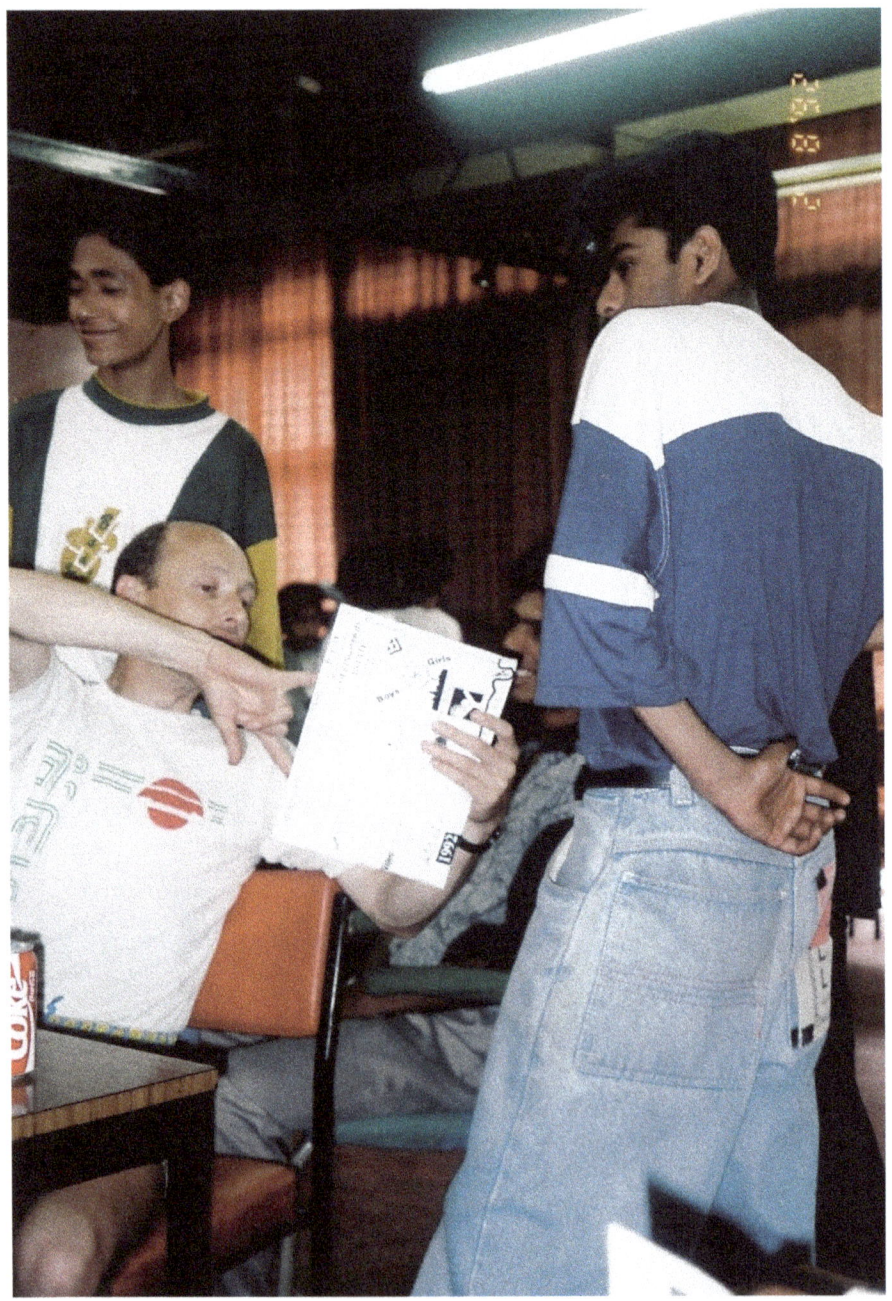

PYO & Collingwood, Joint summer holiday work

East End Photos, Through Mayar's Eyes : Voluntary Sector 1992-1993

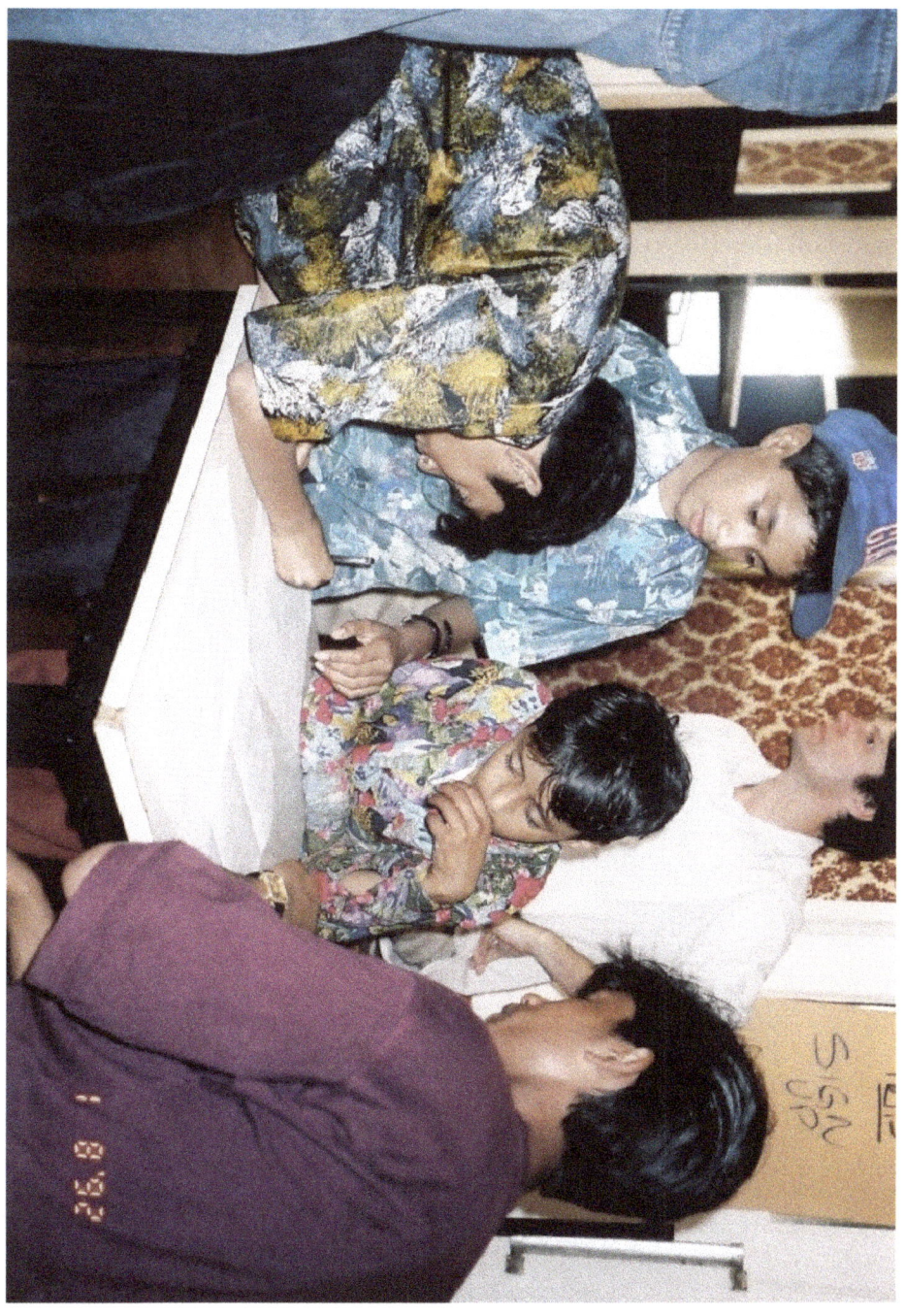

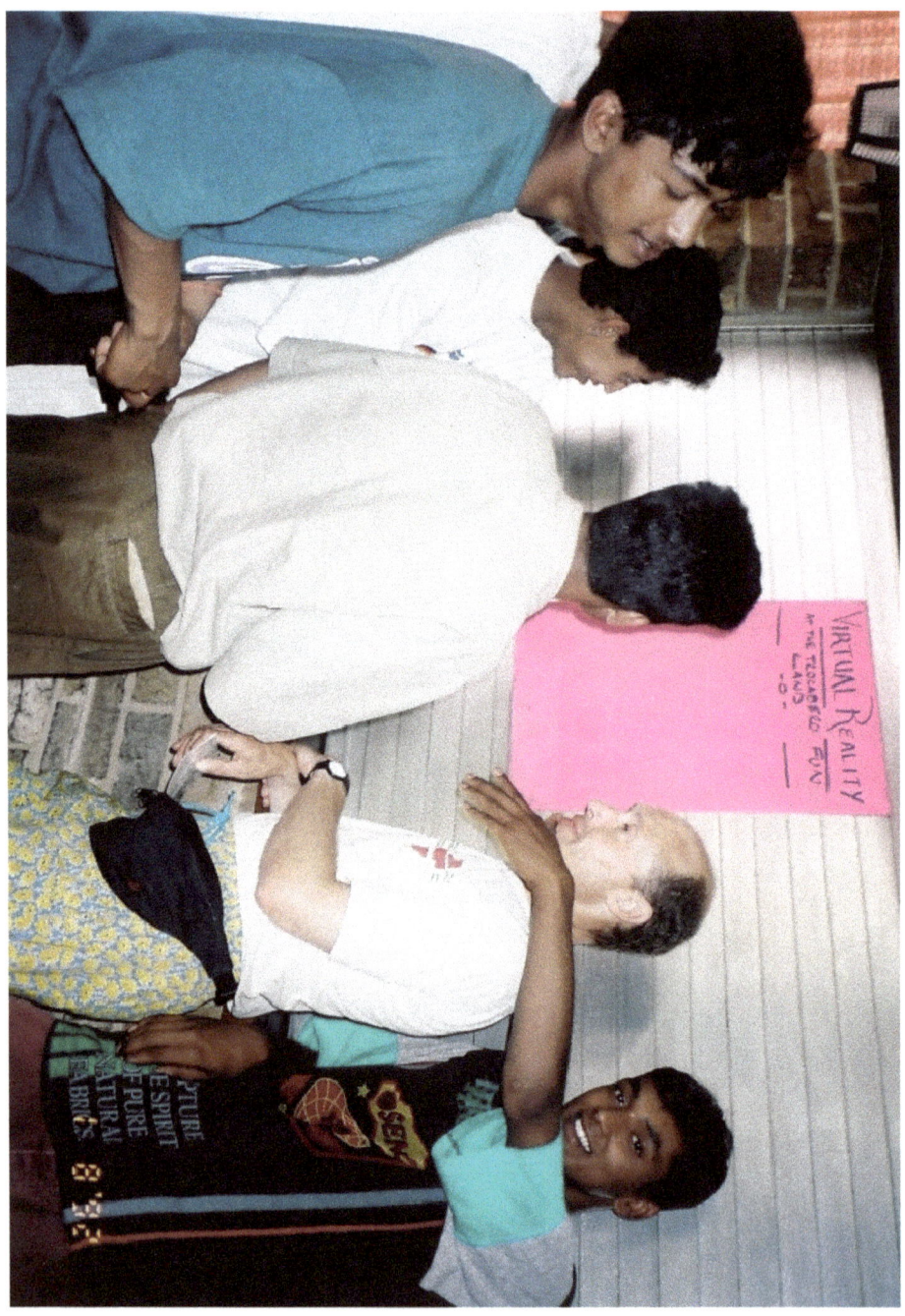

East End Photos, Through Mayar's Eyes : Voluntary Sector 1992-1993

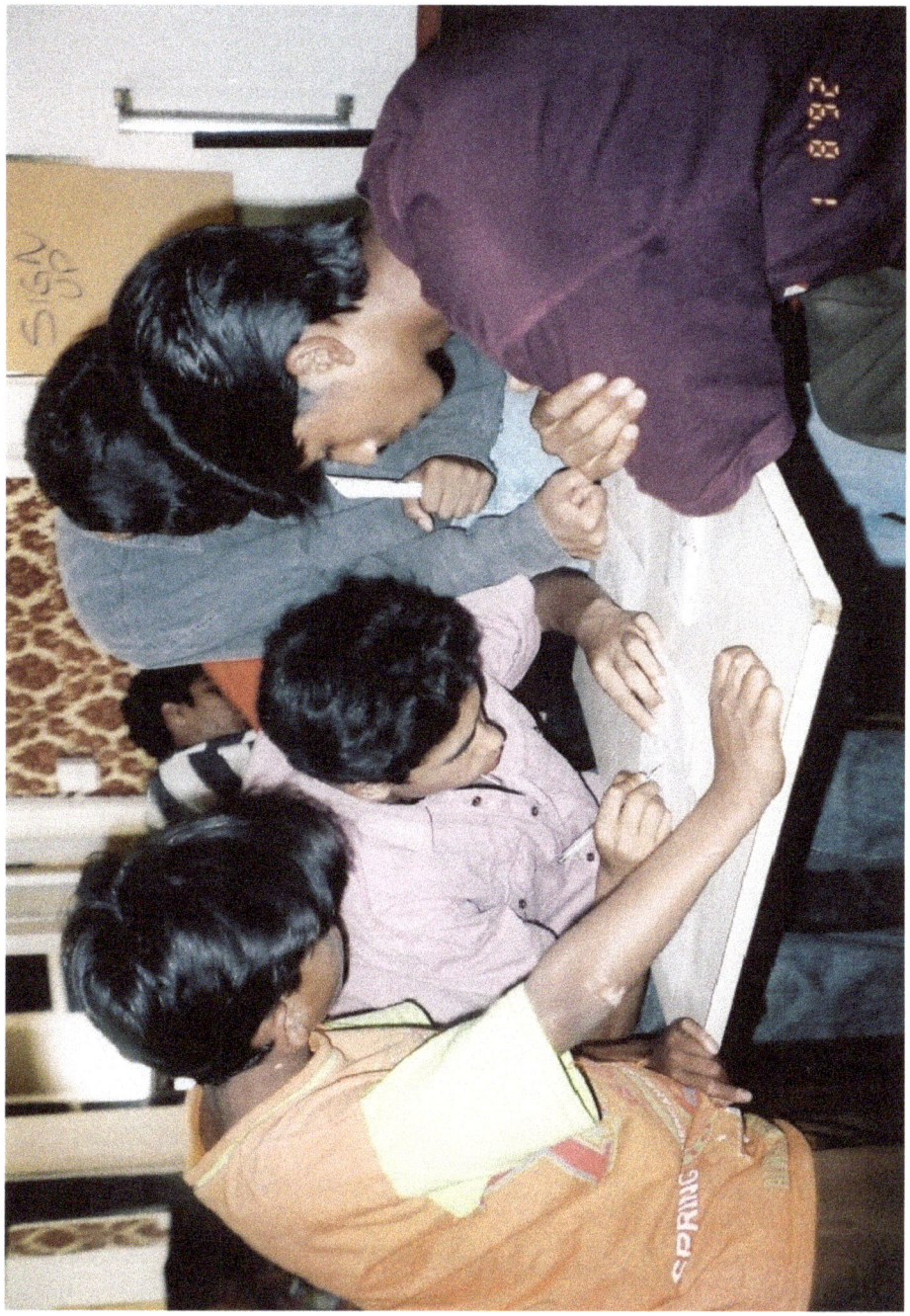

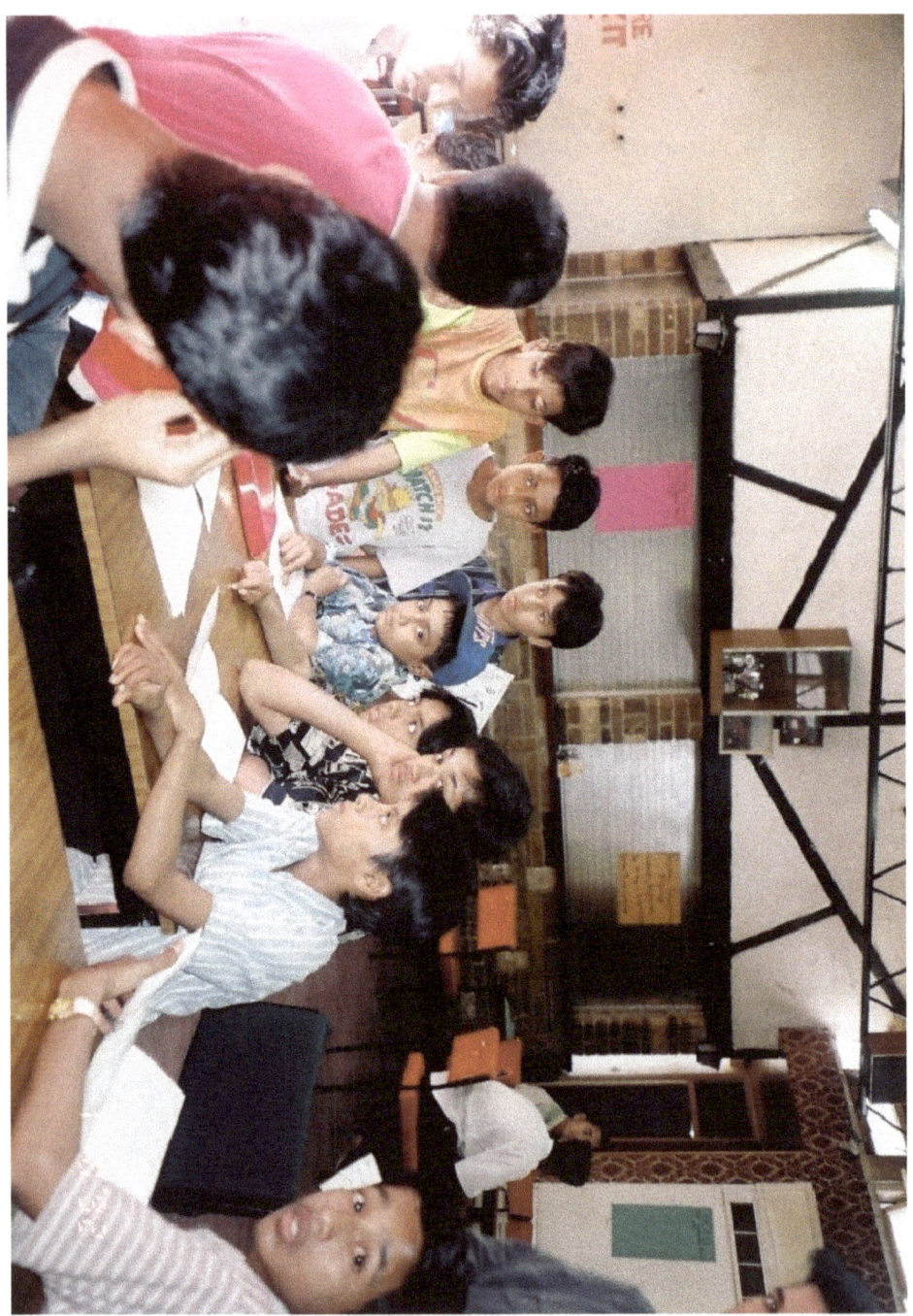

East End Photos, Through Mayar's Eyes : Voluntary Sector 1992-1993

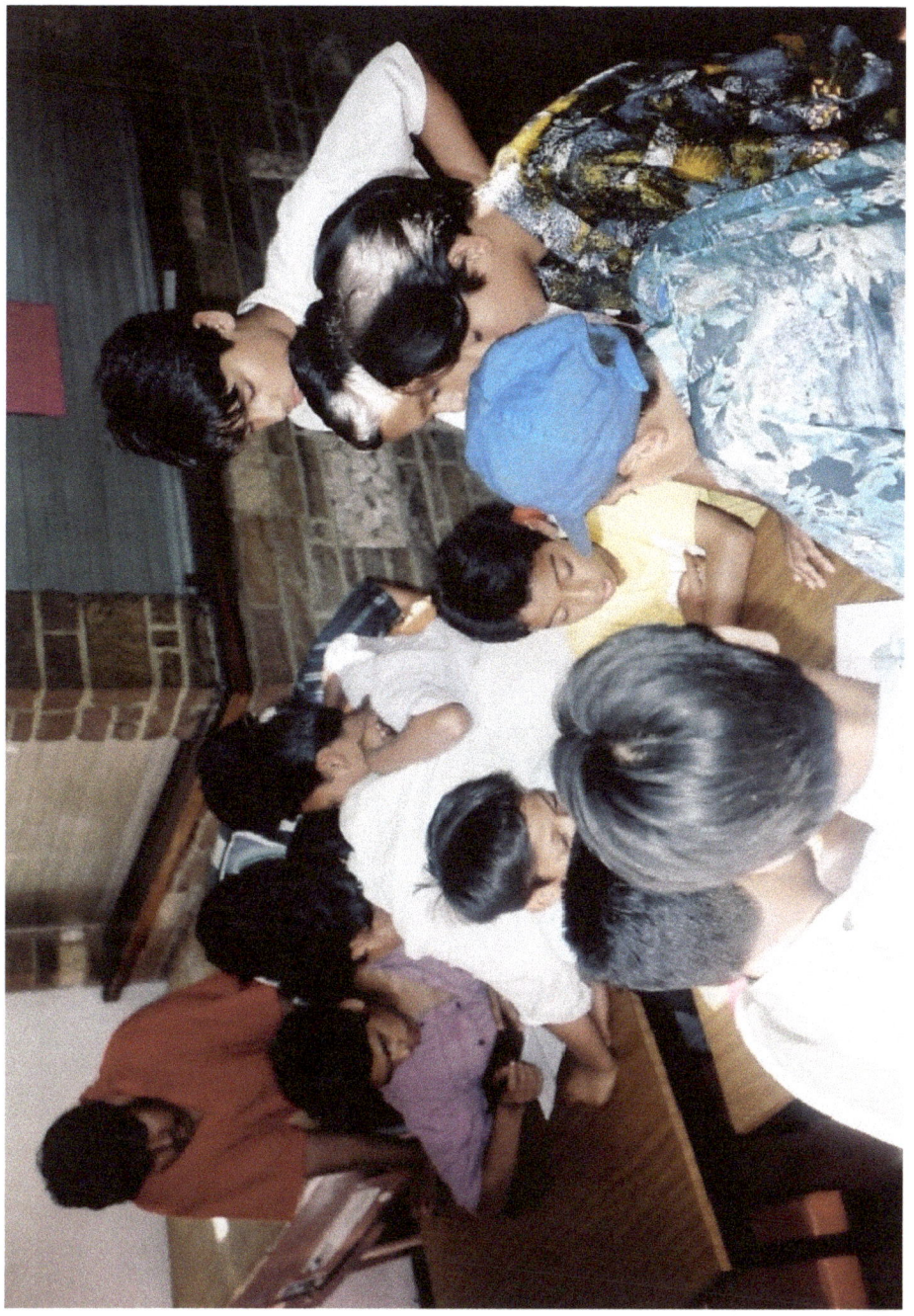

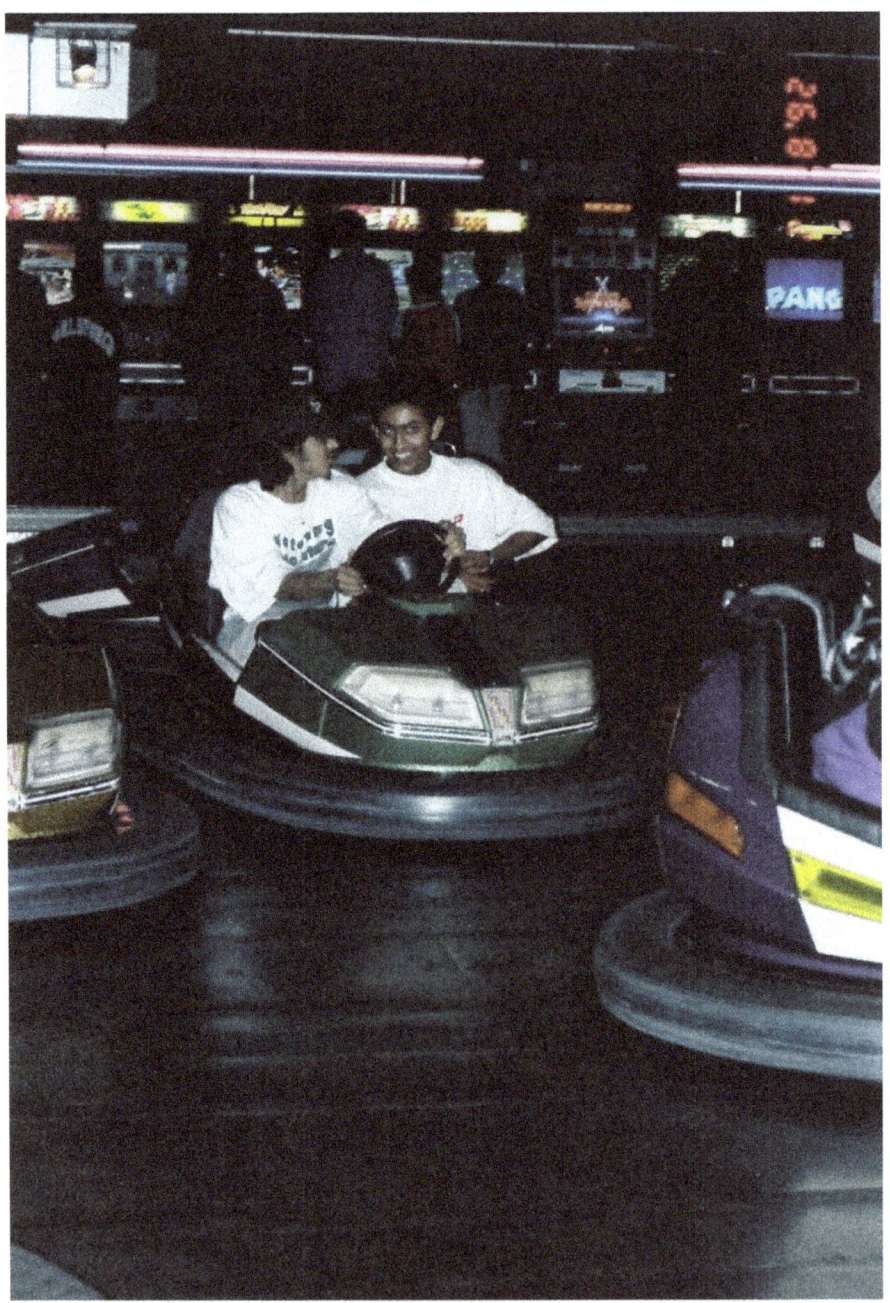

Mizan & Aliur on the bumper car inside Trocedero, West End.

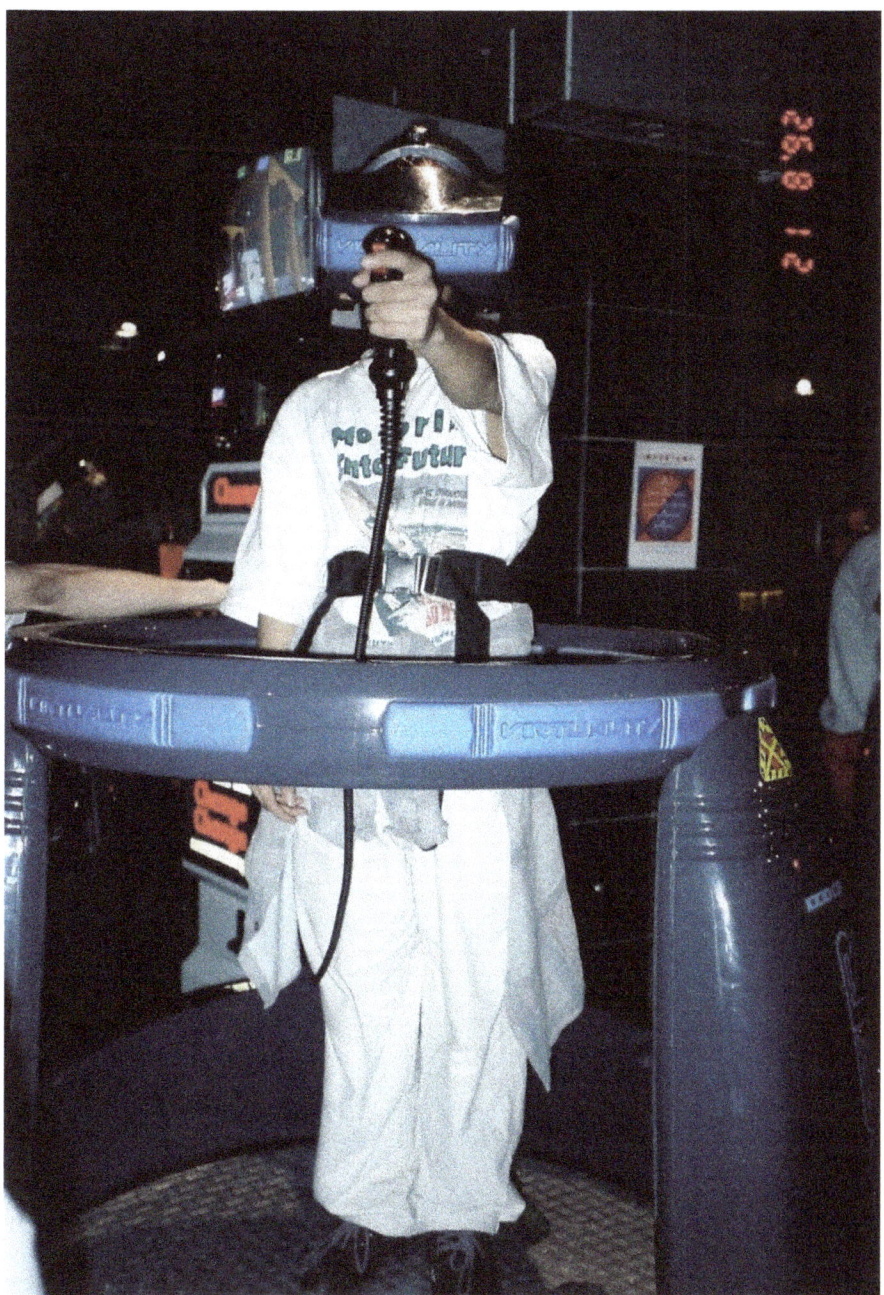

Mizanur Rahman enjoying the virtual game.

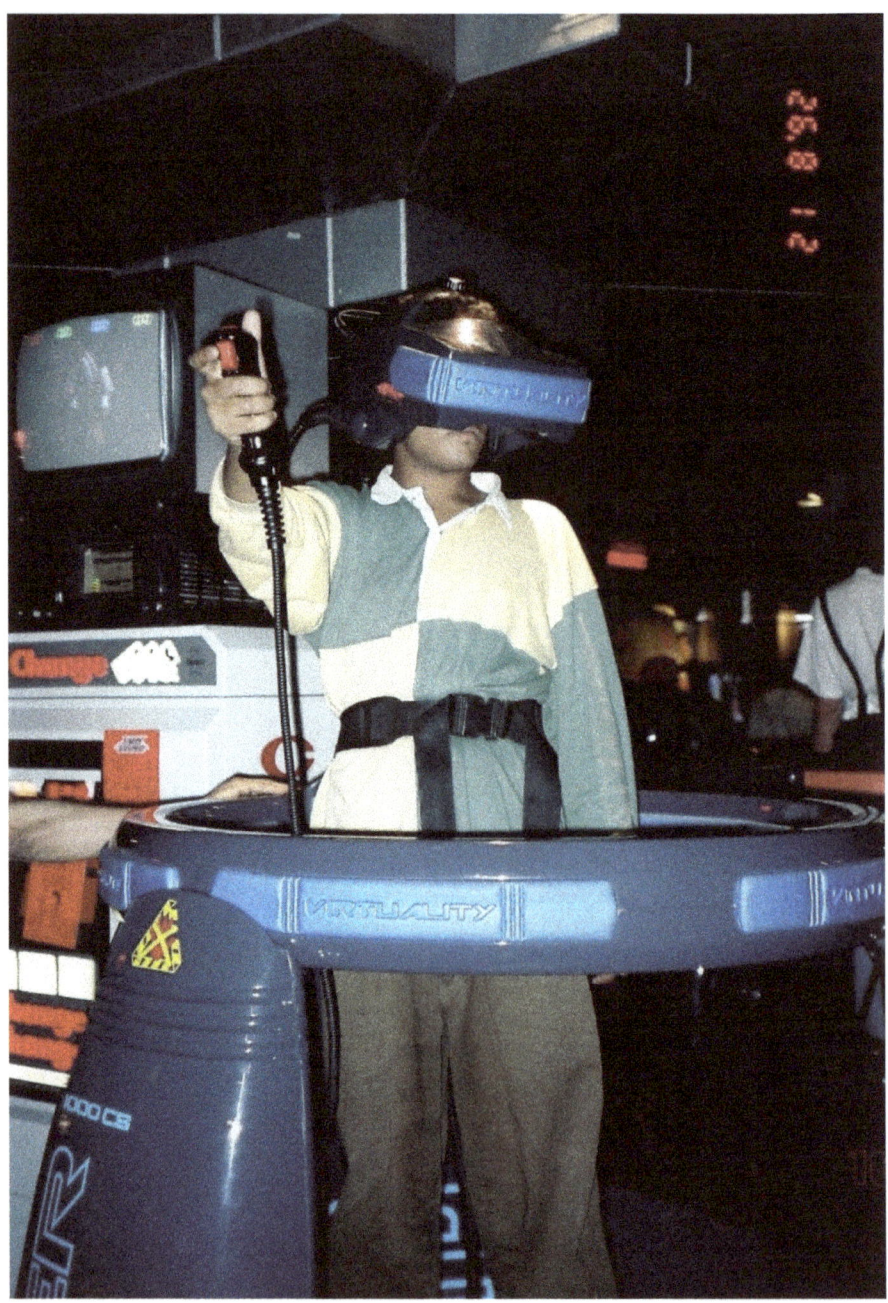

Abdul Munim, having a go at the virtual game at the Trocadero,

www.ingramcontent.com/pod-product-compliance
Lightning Source LLC
Chambersburg PA
CBHW040517220526
45473CB00012B/2896